Apocry

The Writer As Critic Series
Smaro Kamboureli, Series Editor

VIII: Lyric/Anti-lyric
essays on contemporary poetry
Douglas Barbour
ISBN 1-896300-50-2 • $24.95 CDN • $19.95 US

VII: Faking It
Poetics & Hybridity
Critical Writing 1984–1999
Fred Wah
ISBN 1-896300-07-3 • $24.95 CDN • $19.95 US

VI: Readings From the Labyrinth
Daphne Marlatt
ISBN 1-896300-34-0 • $24.95 CDN • $19.95 US

V: Nothing But Brush Strokes
Selected Prose
Phyllis Webb
ISBN 0-920897-89-4 • $24.95 CDN • $19.95 US

IV: Canadian Literary Power
Frank Davey
ISBN 0-920897-57-6 • $24.95 CDN • $19.95 US

III: In Visible Ink
crypto-frictions
Aritha van Herk
ISBN 0-920897-07-X • $24.95 CDN • $19.95 US

II: Signature Event Cantext
Stephen Scobie
ISBN 0-920897-68-1 • $24.95 CDN • $19.95 US

I: Imaginary Hand
George Bowering
ISBN 0-920897-52-5 • $24.95 CDN • $19.95 US

Apocrypha

Further Journeys

(Alberta / Ontario / Newfoundland)

Stan Dragland

The Writer as Critic: IX
Series Editor: Smaro Kamboureli

Copyright © Stan Dragland 2003

All rights reserved. The use of any part of this publication reproduced, transmitted in any form or by any means, electronic, mechanical, recording or otherwise, or stored in a retrieval system, without the prior consent of the publisher is an infringement of the copyright law. In the case of photocopying or other reprographic copying of the material, a licence must be obtained from the Canadian Reprography Collective before proceeding.

Canadian Cataloguing in Publication Data
Dragland, Stan, 1942-
Apocrypha / Stan Dragland.

(The writer as critic ; 9)
Includes bibliographical references and index.
ISBN 1-896300-63-4

1. Dragland, Stan, 1942- 2. Canadian literature (English)—20th century—History and criticism.* I. Title. II. Series: Writer as critic ; 9.

PS8557.R275Z53 2003   C818'.5403   C2002-911460-8
PR9199.3.D735Z462 2003

Editor for the press: Smaro Kamboureli
Cover photo: Cathia Finkel
Cover design: Brenda Burgess

The author wishes to thank the following writers and publishers for permission to quote from their publications: Paul Bowdring, Springer-Verlag, House of Anansi Press, Erin Mouré, John G. Aylen, Agnes Walsh, Phil Hall, Gordon Rodgers, Coach House Press, Jay Macpherson, Random House of Canada, Don McKay, Daphne Marlatt, *The New Quarterly*, Jamila Ismail, Kiyo Kiyooka, Christopher Dewdney, Robert Kroetsch. The passage from Louis Zukofsky's "A" is reprinted with permission of The Johns Hopkins University Press. The excerpt from *The Freedom of the Poet* by John Berryman is copyright © 1976 by Kate Berryman. Reprinted by permission of Farrar, Straus and Giroux, LLC. The map on page 115 is © produced under licence from Her Majesty the Queen in Right of Canada, with permission from Natural Resources Canada. The diagram on page 92 is reprinted by permission of Oxford University Press. Every effort has been made to obtain permission for quoted materials. If there is an omission or error the author and publisher would be grateful to be so informed.

NeWest Press acknowledges the support of the Canada Council for the Arts, The Alberta Foundation for the Arts and the Edmonton Arts Council for our publishing program. We also acknowledge the financial support of the Government of Canada through the Book Publishing Industry Development Program (BPIDP) for our publishing activities.

NeWest Press
201–8540–109 Street
Edmonton, Alberta
T6G 1E6
t: (780) 432-9427
f: (780) 433-3179
www.newestpress.com

1 2 3 4 5 07 06 05 04 03

PRINTED AND BOUND IN CANADA

*For Don McKay and Michael Ondaatje
and for Toby, Simon, and Rachel*

And now for Karl,
whose performance is
for the world
and quiet quiet pleasure

Stan Dragland
at the March Hare
March 2017

Contents

	&	in the world out there	1
A		A fine how d'ya do	2
	&	I'm sitting	7
B		The S.O.L.	9
	&	the wind	11
C		Cod Liver Oil	12
	&	I sent "Cod Liver Oil"	28
D		A Hot Hamburger Sandwich	30
	&	November 11, 1962	34
E		Rescue the Perishing	35
	&	here is the creed	38
F		Police Will Not Turn Handle	39
	&	what I learned	41
G		The Columbia Icefields	45
	&	In the blue Canadian Rockies	48
H		Out-take	49
	&	yes, I passed through	55
I		Bobs Yer Uncle	56
	&	I was at a conference	65
J		"If you can't say something nice,	72
	&	May 1995	74
K		For Crying Out Loud	80
	&	There's a poplar tree	84
L		the fire that breaks from thee then	87
	&	A Big One	92
M		Mountain Railroad	93
	&	I believe	96
N		Les Arnold in London (Ont.)	97

	&	*Foliations* 103
O		Walt Whitman's Niece 104
	&	on the afternoon of November 13, 1992 ... 107
P		*Typing*, Writing, "Racial Memories" 108
	&	it was terribly hot 131
Q		Hortus Conclusus 134
	&	at every session 140
R		Transit 144
	&	Spanner/Wrench 149
S		Sufficient Elasticity 150
	&	jus d'orange? 152
T		Spanner 153
	&	Liselotte was driving me 158
U		Elpenor 160
	&	I was a university student 164
V		Agnes Walsh and Halldór Laxness 165
	&	none of Agnes Walsh's writing 183
W		Twelve Bars 185
	&	I know only one up-side 202
X		The Sound Barrier 203
	&	Amitava Roy didn't sleep 217
YEG–YYT		Edmonton–St. John's, Reading Sujata Bhatt 221
	&	St. John's was a sabbatical destination 228
Z		Burning 230

Sources 241
Acknowledgements 251
Index 253

A

So that were the things words they could say: Light is like night is like us when we meet our mentors.

Louis Zukofsky

B

Nluv, fluv bluv, ffluv biours,
Faith nunfaith kneer beekwl powers
Unfaith naught zwant afaith in all.

Edward Lear

C

What all the name is quakes and moves to you a page of words.

Steve McCaffery

D

Many things are omitted here. The reader who wants to hear about Archimedes taking a bath or about the silver nose of Tycho Brahe can find innumerable books which dwell on these important biographical matters.

Otto Neugebauer

E

... all that time, and right from the first, reading was my darling pleasure.

Bobbie Louise Hawkins

F

[Veroneo] exerted his ultimate stretch of imagination in a monument [The Taj Mahal], to be created in an idiom not his own culture's, to the love for a woman who had been another man's.

John Berryman

G

[I]dentity is a performance.

Margaret Sweatman

H

It's all in the way you act in the world knowing every act is part of the whole fabric.

Mary Kiyoshi Kiyooka / Roy Kiyooka

I

Somewhere slow
poetry is being tender with its alphabet.

Don McKay

J

The taste of salt was a word.
I licked it, named it, rolled it over, loved it.
Then wind, then my ocean, then sky.

Agnes Walsh

K

"When I make a word do a lot of work like that," said Humpty Dumpty, "I always pay it extra."

Lewis Carroll

L

But then language of course is a kind of lullaby.

Charles Simic

M

There is so often something apocryphal about our stories. They are secret stories. They stand outside our own canonical notion of what the story should be.

Robert Kroetsch

N

It was a struggle these days socializing with myself.

Paul Bowdring

O

When it's raining cats and dogs you've got to cut corners because you could get your eyes peeled.

Christopher Dewdney

P & etc.

How to Say Bow Wow
in Chinese: wung wung
in Dutch: haf haf
in Finnish: hau hau
in Icelandic: riff riff
in Portuguese: Au Au
in Russian: Gar Gar
in Spanish: Jau Jau

in the world out there that I sleepwalk through, neither completely in it nor in the other world I seek the key to: a water skier towed by a SeaDoo. I should watch. I should pay attention even to this—as to the lake, to the green of trees on the far shore. That's an elm over there, now that I notice, arching up over the other trees. Survivor of the Dutch Elm plague. A tough tree.

I'm looking through it again, barely in the moment I'm living.

Always moving elsewhere. Always leaving dear friends. Why can't it be here or there, all or nothing, as a shade steps out from this body into the hole it sought? Uneventful descent. The story never lingers on the way down. It rushes to meet the demanding old woman I must be nice nice nice to. She will give me three chances to improve my life. She will let me shake out her feather comforter so the snow will fall. Down there has its own sky! And by the wonder of some folding, some tumbling, inside out, that snow falls on us. Feeling those flakes on our faces, we know this is no mere story.

A

A fine how d'ya do

From Cliché to Archetype is by "Marshall McLuhan with Wilfred Watson." "With." What does that mean? McLuhan has the whole reputation, even now. People with no clear sense of what he thought or said remember "The medium is the message." Who knows about Wilfred Watson, his poems, his plays, his stories? In the reputation sweepstakes, just a few. A few lucky readers know that Wilfred Watson could think and write circles around Marshall McLuhan—not that it makes sense to speak of thinking and writing so. Once in a while the chip is on your shoulder, that's all, and you want to. I'm fighting to brush that chip off this evening, never mind why. I didn't set out to complain, but by god somebody has to shout that *Wilfred Watson's writing hasn't attracted enough attention!*

What I meant to say is that *From Cliché to Archetype*, beginning with "Absurd, Theatre of the," is alphabetical. "Introduction" appears between "Identity—The Culture Hero" and "Jokes." I like this: breaking the order (of argument) in which Introduction always comes first, then healing the break by fitting Introduction smoothly into another order, the alphabet. (Jest joshin, didn't really mean it. See? We like order too.) (But didja notice the title? Backwards, right?)

Yes, I like it, and still I'm circling back to *From Cliché to Archetype*, probing Introduction some more. Can I worry it right out? What if every line introduces *itself*, instanter, *deals out that being indoors each one dwells*. Begin anywhere, dear reader: that's what I want, an anywhere that *Selves—goes itself;* myself *it speaks and spells.* Cries out, and, crying (*What I do is me: for that I came*), breaks and binds a reader's heart. If I could ripple out from every such a pebble, how pedestrian to bother beginning! How sad to want a blanky, beginning, middle, end.

> *You see from 1968 on we really got obsessed with trying to get to a non-narrative prose. Was it possible? Steve and I finally came to see that, no, it was totally impossible. In fact, anybody looking at something, takes a path through it, and that creates a narrative. So the best you can hope for is to present a text which demands of a reader that they organize it themselves. (bpNichol)*

It's not until page 165 of *The Book of Laughter and Forgetting* that Milan Kundera says, "This entire book is a novel in the form of variations. The individual parts follow each other like individual stretches of a journey leading toward a theme, a thought, a single situation, the sense of which fades into the distance." I was enjoying the book up to that point, and I'm sure I would have kept on enjoying it, but suddenly I loved it. A magnet had been introduced to the filings and they snapped into form. Well, the first sentence did that and then the second let go. What I remember liking most about *The Book of Laughter and Forgetting*, except for a hilarious clinical anatomy of the process of laughing, was "This entire book is a novel in the form of variations."

> *The "plot-line" is the drift, which circles back on itself while still moving towards some recognition—*

> *this rather than a plotted crescendo of conflict &*
> *resolution. (Daphne Marlatt)*

Library copies of *Winter Sun* have lost their dust-jackets. No dust in libraries, no jackets. On the inside front flap of the dust-jacket of *Winter Sun*, on behalf of Margaret Avison, somebody says, "The author has arranged her poems for readers who like to skim through a book when they first take it up, since she herself approaches a new book of poetry in this way and would rather find her own groupings than have the poems already grouped for her." This laisser faire would be crucial to me if I were sure that Margaret Avison meant it. If she meant it, in 1960, why not say it in her own words? She must have expressed an opinion to her editor and her editor must have composed a version for the dust-jacket flap. Margaret Avison did say in her own words that "'Literature' results when a) every word is written in the full light of *all* the writer knows; b) the writer accepts the precise limits of what he knows, i.e. distinguishes unerringly (while writing) between what he knows, and what he merely knows about, by reputation or reflected opinion." She wrote that a poem is a "verbal event of absurd independence." If we were looking for masters (but we are not), if we were looking for a guide, we could look to her. What other integrity more nearly approaches the absolute? If so pure a one lets her people go . . .

Dear Reader, would you accept to be so free?

> *"Security?" I marvel to myself "what is that?*
> *Something negative, undead, suspicious and sus-*
> *pecting; an avarice and an avoidance; a self-sur-*
> *rendering meanness of withdrawal; a numerable*
> *complacency and an*

My mother lent *Journeys Through Bookland* to her neighbour and one day later the neighbour brought it back. Their houses were attached so it was easy to return the book. "I can't read this stuff," the neighbour blurted. Mom recounted that ruefully. The maternal pride was hurt; I thought it was funny, and I still do, but I haven't forgotten the heat of that reaction. My book offends against the unities, maybe, but it's plainly written, easy to read. I'm older now, and I know how much is at stake in the relationship between a reader and a book. Or else there's no way in the world I'd risk making things worse by writing this stuff.

I welcome you who read me today, you who read untaught, you with your hunger for words, air to your lungs. Welcome, especially, neighbour, stranger. I don't even know your name but I know you're the very one I want. I'm looking for another life in you. Stand up for amateurs, won't you? Don't leave me to the sophisticates.

> *innumerable cowardice. Who would be 'secure'? Every and any slave. No free spirit ever dreamed of 'security'—or, if he did, he laughed; and lived to shame his dream. No whole sinless sinful sleeping waking breathing human creature ever was (or could be) bought by, and sold for, 'security.' How monstrous and how feeble seems some unworld which would rather have its too than eat its cake!*
> (e. e. cummings)

The opening of the marriage service always moves me deeply. It always fills me—the address to strangers "Dearly Beloved"—absurdly, it always fills me with hope. It's the whole residue of my upbringing in the United Church. The doctrine didn't take, but the residue is potent. *Everything* is in it. I know who is really speaking when the minister says, "Dearly beloved, we are gathered together . . ."

I'm way out here on this island at the extreme eastern edge of the country by choice. If this is exile, I chose it. The silence I find here, when I want to find it, is soothing. But sometimes the urge to break it is overwhelming. I keep wanting to say Dearly Beloved—absurd, facing division and difference everywhere. Dearly Beloved. Dearly Beloved. That's as far as I get. I can't get to the "we." The gathering seems to be beyond me.

I wanted to tell you. Can we sit down together some time? Think of an open-ended appointment, won't you? We have so much to talk through, and it won't be hurried.

&

I'm sitting with Lisa Moore and Kathryn Welbourn in the Heritage Cafe on Duckworth. We're the jury for the Government of Newfoundland & Labrador Book Awards, 2000–2001, non-fiction category, and we're discussing criteria. After months of reading, we'll declare a tie—Patrick O'Flaherty's *Old Newfoundland: A History to 1843* & Mary Pratt's *A Personal Calligraphy*—but now, meeting over, the conversation turns to our own projects. Lisa: a novel, which, by the time we've made our decision, will have turned into *Open*, a book of stories. Kathryn: publishing, editing, and writing her own newspaper, *The Northeast Avalon Times*. & I trot out the latest of my lame accounts of the work-in-progress that will become this book.

Having given so many bad answers to a polite question—What are *you* working on?—I should by now have had the sense to invent and rehearse something plausible. Just to keep the conversation moving. I should have picked something out—life-writing? criticism?—just fill in the conversational blank. But no. Oh, I say, it's a bit of everything.

Who's going to bother looking for a book described like that? Not me. Why can't I blow a bit? I loved writing these pieces, after all. I even like reading them.

Fortunately, I'm talking to curious people. They won't take blah for an answer.

Lisa: Is there any sex?

Kathryn: Are there any maps?

I have a reflex of not answering certain good questions, not in so many words. Over coffee at the Heritage Cafe I didn't say No. I wanted to hold the attention of these good readers a little longer. I wanted to say Maybe, or Why Not? After all, the work in question was a work-in-progress. Just because there were no sex & no maps *so* far . . .

But the time comes to scare out the shadow between question and answer.

Lisa, yes. See page 236 & *passim*. Not what you meant, I know. Nothing like the physical intensity of characters in your own stories. But then all of your writing is a-blush with eros. Eros, one of the old ones. William Carlos Williams wasn't one for fancy Greek words, but he must have been thinking Eros when he said that sex was the engine of his whole life. "I am extremely sexual in my desires," he wrote in the Foreword to his *Autobiography*, "I carry them everywhere and at all times. I think that from that arises the drive which empowers us all. Given that drive, a man does with it what his mind directs. In the manner in which he directs that power lies his secret." Sex is in his writing too, then, all of it. I once heard Williams's New Directions editor give a talk in London, Ontario. The big stumbling block in Bill Williams's life, said James Laughlin, was . . . (embarrassed pause) . . . *dames*. An American word from a bygone era. Humphrey Bogart as Philip Marlowe. Ray Walston as Luther Billis, with horny sailor ensemble, in *South Pacific*: "There is nothing like a dame . Nothing . in the . world." Williams was prolific, especially for a doctor, but maybe he would have stumbled less if he'd written even more. Myself, I'm writing as much as ever I can.

"The Territory Is Not The Map," Kathryn. So Jack Spicer says. But "a paragraph is a kind of map too." So Erin Mouré says. As is a sentence. And see page 115.

B

The S.O.L.

I grew up in Alberta, so ignorant that for years I had no idea what I needed most in my life: poetry. Specifically, I needed poetry that sang the coyote, the gopher, the grain elevator, the alkali slough, the binder twine, the Magma. Add crop rotation, prairie wool, and freight rates and you have the subjects par excellence of Saskatchewan's greatest poet, Sarah Binks. Yes, the poetry of Sarah Binks changed my life.

A lot of the credit goes to Paul Hiebert, who discovered the "Sweet Songstress of Saskatchewan" and celebrated her "peculiar genius" in his critical biography. A reprint of this classic is fabulous news to devout Binksians like myself. It means that new generations of readers may thrill to the pungency of Sarah's verse. No doubt there will once again be fierce debate between the Binksians and the Antis, as when I was growing up ignorant (but with hand-curled hair) in southeastern Alberta. I'll never forget the time a group of us partisans were taunted thus: What's the difference between Sarah Binks's poetry and a pile of manure? How could we help but ask?

Just the straw, that's all.

Do as I say and not as I do, we shouted as one, and flung the wretch into the back of Glenn Kenny's pickup. Out at Glenn's farm we changed his mind behind the pig barn. We explained to him Sarah's wonderful line, "Send out the S.O.L. my hearties." Ah, youth. Now I realize there was a compliment buried in the seeming taunt, but isn't it just like a group of green minds to confuse form and content?

Changed my life? That's not the half of it. Everything I am, Sarah's poetry made me. Ole, the hired man; Rover; Steve Grizzlykick (Stemka Gryczlkaeiouc); Mathilda Schwantzhacker, Henry Welkin—all the vivid personages of Sarah's life and art in both her Pre- and Post-Regina periods—they have fertilized my mind. It moved me deeply to discover, after my father passed away, that his enthusiasm had all but matched my own. Among his effects we found an aerosol can labelled "Prof. Willoughby's World-Famous Bullshit Repellent." In honour of his memory and in tribute to Sarah's poetry, I never use it.

&

the wind is so strong in southern Alberta (Dad used to say) that all the barbs on all the barbed-wire fences point to the east.

C

Cod Liver Oil

for The Ship Inn, St. John's, Newfoundland

I

Here I am in St. John's, reading about cod liver oil in your poem, Gordon, and my mind slips away from Newfoundland, out across most of Canada, all the way back to Stettler, in the heart of Alberta, laps of time unfolding as I go, until I'm a new boy in Miss Hansen's Grade Six class once again. Why did I always think of Miss Hansen as Scottish? Hansen isn't a Scottish name.

Miss Hansen had a Canadian accent, but that didn't matter. Canada had no grip on our imagination then. Your nationality was where your father's people came from, so I was Norwegian whenever anyone asked. Miss Hansen could have been Scottish even if she didn't sound like it. But it was *Miss* Hansen. Her maiden name was Scandinavian, like mine. Maiden name: odd phrase for a name taken from a father. Old maid: the uncharitable way of referring to Miss Hansen. Half a century later it finally occurs to me that she'd be Scottish on her mother's side.

It was the kilt she often wore, with the special long pin to keep it closed, and the Cairngorm brooch she always pinned to her blouse on the days she wore the kilt. Miss Hansen was very proud of that brooch and she taught whatever she was proud of, whatever she loved, whether she intended to or not. She taught us her Cairngorm brooch and Rosa Bonheur's *The Horse Fair*, and the brooch and the painting have been with me all these years, and not just as items, facts, but as treasure, alive and glowing—and buried, Gordon, mostly buried until now. The stone in that Cairngorm brooch was a little brighter than amber. It was almost golden, but I see it as the bloom of a brooch made in the shape of a thistle, flower of Scotland, so it should be purple. All beauty and prickle, the thistle was surely Miss Hansen's flower. It was in her class that I learned to sing

> The thistle, shamrock, rose entwine
> The Maple Leaf forever.

I loved that woman.

―◄o►―

My family had moved from the Peace River Country to Edmonton, and then, six months later, to Stettler, so I was adrift again. Big school, no friends. I could tell it was going to be better than Edmonton, anyway, where school was terrifying. I was glad when the measles kept me home there, even though I had to stay in the dark and rest my eyes. The most my mother would let me do was cut out pictures of Princess Elizabeth to paste in a scrapbook. Her father, King George, died on February 6 of 1952. The princess became Queen Elizabeth on June 2, and my scrapbook followed her right through to the coronation. From my Grade Five school room, two kids were released early every day so other kids wouldn't beat them up. Nobody wanted to beat me up. Nobody paid me any attention, but violence was always in the air. Older kids called younger kids "kid," with a sharp edge of automatic scorn in the tone. Once I did meet a troll in the McKinnon Ravine. He wouldn't let me pass, nohow, and I was no Billy Goat Gruff.

I watched the kids on the school playground in Stettler, pretending not to watch, pretending I had lots to think about. I could see that they weren't so rough as the kids in Edmonton, so that was something. Nobody knew yet that my mother was teaching in the high school that was joined to the elementary school by a breezeway. They weren't going to single me out and tease me because of that, not yet. Once in a while, before school or at recess, my eyes met those of another boy who seemed to have lots to think about. We drifted together after a couple of days. He spoke with a drawl I'd never heard before. His name was David Ray and his parents were from Texas. He and his mother were living in the trailer court for now, while his father was travelling the province. Something to do with oil. Only poor people lived in trailers, I knew that. But David didn't look poor, and when he invited me to the trailer that didn't seem poor either. There were built-in fish tanks at the bedroom end of it, right at eye-level, and there were tropical fish in the tank, the first I'd ever seen. I would have liked just to look and look, but David had to tell me everything he knew about his fish, and he knew a lot—species, habitat, diet, everything—all in his droning drawl. I pretended to be interested, but, really, a person might as well be in school. Pretty soon I started pretending to be busy so I wouldn't have to go over there and listen to David lecture.

On the days when Miss Hansen wore her Cairngorm brooch we could hear the bagpipes in her voice, we could actually see the heather waving on her wide, flat face, so animated when something interested her, and so mean-looking in repose. It made you shiver just to glimpse her then. That stony face alone would have kept us in line. The kilt wrapped her thick body neatly. The thick legs you could see beneath the kilt looked just the way legs should look. They hardly tapered at the ankles, but met her Oxfords suddenly.

Miss Hansen's face lit up for Rosa Bonheur. She told us all about Rosa Bonheur's unconventional life—unusual for a woman to stay single and earn her own living in the mid-nineteenth century, unusual to wear pants, and actually shocking to ride a horse astride, because at that time women were expected to ride sidesaddle. But people let her do all that because she was married to her painting. "Art is an absorbent,—a tyrant," she wrote. "It demands heart, brain, soul, body, the entireness of its votary. Nothing less will win its highest favour. I wed art. It is my husband—my world—my life-dream—the air I breathe. I know nothing else—feel nothing else—think nothing else. My soul finds in it the most complete satisfaction. I married art. . . . What could I do with any other husband?" Wow! We only got the gist of that from Miss Hansen, but we could tell from her that Rosa Bonheur was special.

Miss Hansen didn't mention Nathalie Micas, Rosa Bonheur's longtime companion. Maybe she didn't know about Nathalie Micas, or about Anna Klumpke, the American companion of the last years, whom Rosa Bonheur referred to as her wife. In a photograph of 1882, Nathalie Micas and Rosa Bonheur look just like Gertrude Stein and Alice B. Toklas of a later age. Rosa is wearing the Legion of Honour medal that the Empress Eugénie presented her. The little dog on Nathalie's lap is wearing a necklace and staring at the camera every bit as fiercely as the two women.

◄o►

Look at those horses, Miss Hansen said, holding up a reproduction of Rosa Bonheur's *The Horse Fair*.

Does anyone know what kind of horses those are? No? Those are Percherons. P-e-r-c-h-e-r-o-n, Percheron. Those are draft horses, which is to say working horses, for pulling heavy loads. See how big and strong they look?

They look dangerous.

Yes, Wendy, it looks like it would be a job to control them, doesn't it. You can feel the strength of those horses, can't you? That's how realistic they are. It feels like there could be a stampede. For the life of me, I can't understand why anyone would complain that Rosa Bonheur couldn't paint trees—see the trees in the background here? Who wants to look at the trees anyway? It's the horses you want to look at.

Those are good trees.

I am very much inclined to agree with you, Wendy. Now. Does anyone know how large this painting is?

About one foot by two feet?

No, Leo, that is the size of this picture. This is a print, a reproduction of the real painting. Anybody else? No?

That painting is ninety-six and one-half inches high and one hundred and ninety-nine and one-half inches wide. It would cover that whole wall.

She waved at the blackboard side of the classroom, smiling at the gasps. I watched the blackboard as if *The Horse Fair* might come alive up there while Miss Hansen spoke about how Rosa Bonheur took the Paris Salon by storm with *The Horse Fair* in 1853, and how her career was established from that moment on, how important people were always coming to visit her studio, where she always had animals living in, even a lion that roamed free, yes, that's right, because she liked animals better than people, and even Buffalo Bill came to visit, because naturally he liked horses too and was in

Paris with his Wild West Show, including Sitting Bull and Annie Oakley, and a Canadian was even in the show for a while, did we know who that might be? No? Gabriel Dumont, who was Louis Riel's general, and such a good general that he might have whipped Sir John A. Macdonald in the Rebellion of 1885, but that's another story. And Buffalo Bill, whose real name was William Cody, sent Rosa Bonheur—all the way from America—sent her two wild mustangs that it turned out no one at Rosa Bonheur's place could tame, so finally he had to send a couple of cowboys over to break those horses, but they really weren't the kind of horses Rosa Bonheur liked best anyway. She liked the big work horses, like the Percherons in the picture here, and she liked the big oxen that were used for ploughing in France at that time, and Rosa Bonheur's first great picture was called *Ploughing in the Nivernais*, and was a picture of those oxen plowing. So those wild mustangs that Buffalo Bill sent all the way from America had to go with his Wild West Show again. And Rosa Bonheur painted a wonderful picture of Buffalo Bill which Buffalo Bill loved so much that when he was travelling, and word came that his house in Wyoming was burning, you know what he did? He telegraphed his wife to save the Rosa Bonheur painting of him and let everything else burn. That's how much Buffalo Bill thought of Rosa Bonheur.

—◄o►—

I don't know about you, Gordon, but until Grade Six, there were two subjects that I drew every time I felt like drawing, which was quite often. I never found lack of talent at all discouraging. I drew a house, viewed from catty-corner so you could see the side, which to me was the front so I put the door in there and a path from the door curving down to the bottom of the page and widening as it went. I put a single window in the front, which to me was the side, with a cross in the window to divide it into panes. I put a chimney on the roof with a curl of smoke coming out of it. I drew a horizon line to intersect the house so it wouldn't just float on the page, and a sun in the sky with rays radiating out from it, and a few relaxed Vs for distant birds.

Or else I made two hills out of two lines. One started just below halfway up the right-hand side of the page and arced to the bottom just over halfway across. The other hill line joined the first not quite at the bottom of the page. I put a tree on the first hill, with a tuft of grass at the base. I put scratches here and there on both hills to show that they were grassed. Branches shot out alternately from the trunk of the tree, and twigs branched alternately from the branches. This was no particular kind of tree. I put in the leaves last—a lot of curved pencil lines that didn't attach anywhere. When it came to leaves, I was an impressionist. Finally, I put my usual sun and distant birds into the sky.

Over and over, the same two scenes. It was all I ever thought to do, except now and then an airplane, but I had the same trouble attaching the wing to the fuselage that I did making the tree grow naturally out of the hill. Once I saw an airplane sewn in cloth and stuffed, and it looked every bit as likely to fly as my airplane on paper.

Again and again, the house and the hills. I can reproduce them exactly today as I did when I was in Grade Six, my talent standing at exactly the same level now as then. But under the influence of Miss Hansen and Rosa Bonheur, I spent much of Grade Six drawing horses.

There were horses on my uncle's ranch within sight of the Cypress Hills in southeastern Alberta. A few years later, when I spent three weeks on the ranch, Uncle Jimmy caught Midge for me and got me aboard in the field near the house and left me alone to ride her all afternoon. First time on a horse, bareback.

Just lay the bridle across her neck on this side when you want her to turn left, or else lay the bridle across her neck on this side, see, when you want her to go right. Pull back on the reins when you want her to stop. No need to say whoa, though you can if you want. Got that?

I guess so. Oh. How do I get her started?

Just loosen the reins and go *tch tch tch* and dig your heels in here.

Where, here?

That's right. Right in here. Okay?

I guess so.

Good. So we'll see you later then.

It wasn't long before Midge wanted a drink at the dugout. I balanced okay by leaning back when she stretched her neck down to the water, but when she reared to release her hooves from the mud I fell off. There I was, no way to get back on. I wasn't going to walk that big horse up to the barbed wire and try mounting from the top strand.

I never had much luck with real horses, but I didn't need a real horse in 1953. Miss Hansen told us that Rosa Bonheur studied horses in the livestock markets of France and, with Buffalo Bill's permission, in his Wild West Show, but she didn't mention the trips to slaughterhouses to find out what was underneath those beautiful muscles. "One must know what is under their skin," she said. "Otherwise your animal will look like a mat rather than a tiger." It was hard work to make animals look real on canvas, apparently, but I didn't think any of that applied to me. I copied my horses from Red

Ryder comics, and I was very happy with my work.

My best horse ever was on my desk the day the school inspector came. I was especially proud of the hindquarters, with the muscles so beautifully shaded in. Miss Hansen conducted the inspector up and down the aisles to see the art on display. When they paused by my side, I looked up to receive the admiration I fully expected and surprised them both suppressing grins. Alone, Miss Hansen would never have lost control of her face, but hilarity is contagious. I looked at my horse again. Maybe the proportions weren't exactly right. Maybe not, but that horse still looked good to me.

—◄o►—

Miss Hansen read us two books, a chapter a day, one in each part of the year. She read *Ben-Hur* and *Anne of Green Gables*. For a long time, remembering only the chariot race in *Ben-Hur*, I assumed that the first was for the boys and the second for the girls. But I suspect that my memory of the race comes from the Charlton Heston movie, because now that I look for the first time at Lew Wallace's horribly overwritten, sentimental "tale of the Christ," I just wonder how Miss Hansen can ever have held us with it. As if life wasn't hard enough for Jews in Roman times, Ben-Hur's mother and sister contract leprosy. "Lepers, lepers!" exclaims Ben-Hur when a page later he finds out about the affliction. "They—my mother and Tirzah—they lepers! How long, how long, O Lord!" Until about fifty pages later, as it turns out, when the Christ cures them. I don't think Leo Fix was listening very carefully when Miss Hansen read us this stuff. The essay he wrote on *Ben-Hur* was all about leopards. Miss Hansen read it aloud to us and we laughed our heads off.

Anne of Green Gables was something else. I loved every bit of it. I couldn't wait to hear another chapter. It was the writing, Gordon, just as it's the tautness of your poem about cod liver oil that shocks me into remembering.

So here I am in Miss Hansen's class, an eleven-year-old boy enthralled, totally identified with a paper girl of about my own age, looking out of her eyes as she surveys the new dresses Marilla has spread out on the bed in the Gable Room:

> One was of snuffy coloured gingham which Marilla had been tempted to buy from a peddler the preceding summer because it looked so serviceable; one was of black-and-white checked sateen which she had picked up at a bargain counter in the winter; and one was a stiff print of an ugly blue shade which she had purchased that week at a Carmody store.

Now listen, Gordon. Listen to another artist at her work. Listen to the magic made when the right words are wedded. I didn't know it then, but rhythms shaped like these would bury *Anne of Green Gables* in my heart: "She had made them up herself, and they were all made alike—plain skirts fulled tightly to plain waists, with sleeves as plain as waist and skirt and tight as sleeves could be." I never cared what I wore at the age of eleven, and yet I passionately wanted those plain dresses embellished at the very least with puffed sleeves, because Anne wanted puffed sleeves. My satisfaction was immense when Matthew smoked and smoked the pipe that Marilla found so filthy until he figured out why Anne looked unlike the other girls and then smoked some more until he figured out how to do something about it.

Everything that happened that year happened once. There was no pattern, because I never thought to look for it. There was Rosa Bonheur and there was *Ben-Hur*. There was *Ben-Hur* and there was *Anne of Green Gables*. There was *Anne of Green Gables* and the Cairngorm brooch. There was me and there was David Ray. Nothing joined, nothing overlapped. There was Leo Fix's leopards and there was Miss Hansen's inquisition when somebody stole twenty-five cents from Wendy Wilson's coat in the cloakroom. You could tell Miss Hansen suspected Barry McQuaig. He was the funniest kid in the school, but he had a bad reputation with adults. So we all had to stay after school while Miss Hansen tried to terrify the truth out of him.

2

In 1851, Rosa Bonheur had already begun her eighteen months of preparatory work for *The Horse Fair*, Giuseppe Verdi's *Rigoletto* premiered in Venice, and the Three-Penny Beaver, Canada's first postage stamp and the first pictorial stamp ever, was issued. And in 1851, says John E. Maunder in *Newfoundland Museum Notes* #2,

> the prototype of all future "international exhibitions," or "world fairs," was opened at the colossal, purpose-built "Crystal Palace" in London. Countries from all over the globe sent exhibits extolling the virtues of their respective cultural and industrial products and resources. But, alas, Newfoundland's contribution—a *single bottle* of

cod liver oil!—was decidedly undistinguished. The local press responded with derision.

You can see why they would. You might suspect that whoever was in charge of representing Newfoundland in the Crystal Palace had not gone out of his way. The Great Exhibition of the Works and Industry of All Nations had over six million visitors, and one hundred and fifty years later people are still talking about the Crystal Palace, so that was a big opportunity lost. Right?

I'm not so sure. I wonder if that single bottle of cod liver oil wasn't just the thing. I am very much inclined, in fact, to think it was brilliant. There certainly are times when you want your culture and your industrial products and resources displayed in all their rich variety. That was the norm in the Exhibition of 1851, which is to say that no other country had distilled itself into the contents of a single small bottle. And Mr. Maunder doesn't mention the talker. He says nothing about the Newfoundlander who accompanied the bottle. All that's needed is a talker to open it up, you see. A sniff, a taste. Everything comes out in a story then. Along the branching lines of story, however single the source, there is *nothing* you can't reach. After all, my whole story comes out of a bottle, a barrel to be exact—a barrel of cod liver oil that I discovered after moving to Newfoundland. I found it in *Floating Houses,* Gordon, in the poem you called "Recipe," your formula for surviving "regular random disasters." It was the last part that set me dreaming:

> Most
> of all, hold your health: keep a
> barrel for cod livers. Let them
> stand and froth all through the

brewing summer. Dip out a fingerful. Taste the pungent oil, the true tonic of this shore.

No wonder Charles Dickens was overwhelmed by the Great Exhibition. The catalogue of objects displayed, after all, from the Koh-i-noor diamond to an expanding hearse, filled three massive volumes, each five hundred pages in length. Here in the Medical section is a display of the latest bleeding instruments, "substitutes for leeches," the card says. Here are the artificial arms and here the false teeth, one of them boasting "a compensating swivel which allows the wearer to yawn without displacing both upper and lower sets." What'll they think of next! Here is a "medical walking-stick" containing medicines, surgical instruments, and an enema, and right next to it a false nose made of silver. And here on this small pedestal table is a bottle, a single bottle of, hmm, of cod liver oil. Cod liver oil! That's it. Pick it up, raise it to the light. Sit down, take a load off, listen while Mr. Casey the shopkeeper "visits a barrel filled with rotting cod livers and takes a mussel shell and dips up a measure of the oil and drinks it down." So Mr. Casey's day begins, with a measure of the true tonic of this shore, this essence of the cod, "Neptune's sheep, the only real fish in the sea," and so the story begins. You'll be captive by that Crystal Palace stall for hours, for days. You'll have to tear yourself away ages before the long dream of the new found land has unfolded to where the plenty, the plentitude of cod has been pissed away. If everything can be put into a bottle, you know, then everything can be poured out again.

◄o►

Once a week, courtesy of the Alberta government, Miss Hansen dispensed us a cod liver oil pill, true tonic for mainlanders. Most of the others hated it. They were probably thinking fish and livers, either one of which is enough to make an eleven-year-old gag. But cod liver oil was neither fish nor liver to me. <u>Cod Liver Oil</u>! <u>Cod Liver Oil</u>—you can chant it. I was used to spoonfuls of cod liver oil from the bottle my mother kept at home, and I always bit into my pill to get that slippery taste.

All of this, Gordon—Miss Hansen, everything—gone, lost, then suddenly found in your poem.

When Newfoundland joined Confederation, we were still in northern Alberta, in Grimshaw. They marched us from the school to the Elks Hall for the ceremony, and I can still see it. I can see verticals on the stage of the Elks Hall. Some of them were people and some of them were flags. I stood on that same stage once myself. I wasn't supposed to be standing. I was supposed to be dancing the highland fling with four of my Grade Three classmates, but I forgot the last step, so I stood there with my face on fire, grinning at the audience. The audience grinned back, much better entertained by my embarrassment than they had been by my dancing. Miss MacKenzie was the teacher. She *was* Scottish, and she taught highland dancing, and that's why some of us happened to be dancing the highland fling on the same northern Alberta stage where Newfoundland was welcomed into Canada.

I was savouring my cod liver oil pill, as usual, holding the oil on my tongue as long as I could and then squeezing out the last of it with little bites on the skin of the pill, when Miss Hansen swept up from behind, hauled me roughly out of my desk, and whacked me three times on the backside with her yardstick.

Don't you *dare* make faces in my classroom! she hissed.

I wasn't!

And don't you dare talk back to me, young man!

The yardstick didn't hurt, but the indignity did—spanked on the bum like a baby, and for something I didn't even do! Not fair!

That's what I told my mother at noon, when I also informed her that I wasn't going back to school again, ever.

You're sure you weren't making faces?

No! Why would I make faces? I was just eating my pill!

Eating it?

Yes, eating it.

Well, anyway, you have to go back. You can't stay home from school.

I don't care! I'm not going!

The iron had entered into my soul. But my mother was adamant. She said I had to go back after my music lesson, which would make me a little late, but that she'd go and talk to Miss Hansen. I had thought the world of Miss Hansen, she knew, so she could tell this was serious. She had no problem with discipline. She had her own reputation for toughness, but she was always fair. Her students teased me because they liked her.

One of the pieces in my piano book that year, the second-last year of piano lessons for me, as one rebellion succeeded another, was "La donna è mobile," from *Rigoletto*. I liked to make my sister laugh by singing the English words out of the book in my best operatic soprano, and with grand gestures appropriate to a prairie boy who was not going to see an actual opera for another fourteen years.

> Woman is changeable
> Light as a feather

> False as fair weather
> Who can believe her?

My piano book didn't mention that the aria is sung by a notorious seducer in a tragedy.

First *this* happened that year, then *that* happened. Nothing connected. Miss Hansen might have lived at school, for all I knew or cared. She was there in the morning when I arrived, she was there in the afternoon when I left. I never saw her anywhere in town. I had no idea where she lived, never heard anything that so much as hinted that she had a private life.

I was ten minutes late for school and out of breath from running up the stairs. I closed the classroom door behind me and turned to see Miss Hansen flashing me the most radiant smile I had ever seen. Such a big, big smile, just for me. I smiled back, thrilled, and that was that.

&

I sent "Cod Liver Oil" to my mother in Alberta. I knew she'd remember Miss Hansen & I thought she might like to see what my most difficult year in elementary school had turned into. Macular degeneration had contracted Mom's vision to where she could just barely watch television by sitting sidelong to the set & peering out of the corner of her eye. She was still in her own house, having lived her patterns there long enough to manage for herself, but she couldn't read. One of the great joys of her life. Now she was a client of the CNIB. They sent her a collapsible white cane with a retractable ice pick & enrolled her in their lending library of talking books. My sister Betty was now picking up Mom's mail. She read Mom the story.

I thought you hated that woman, Mom said when I saw her next. Yes, that too. But she was the only teacher who held my interest, the only oasis of terror & delight between Grades One & Twelve, the single contradiction in my own experience of the cynical opinion that schools are for nothing more than shaping unruly individuals into docile citizens. I have only to think of Miss Hansen & I'm back in her classroom, sparking to that old electricity.

Miss Hansen seemed almost omniscient to me, but she did miss a few things. She had no trouble with Rainer Ganz, even though she never passed him. He stayed in Grade Six as a sort of trusty until he was old enough to quit school. His head wouldn't hold much but he was content to wait out his sentence quietly in the back seat of his row. Once in a while he'd undo his pants & show his wares to Wendy Wilson (which may have contributed to Wendy's precocity in Grade Seven, when she sent Valentine's cards to half a dozen of us, each pledging "all my love"), but Miss Hansen never noticed.

Miss Hansen made so much of the time I spent with her that very little of it is gone. Now that I know that so much precious life just evaporates, how can I help but love her?

Hand-curled hair

D

A Hot Hamburger Sandwich

Driving from small-town Alberta down the west coast through Washington and Oregon, into California. Sea Lion Caves, Trees of Mystery, Knott's Berry Farm, Disneyland. Every restaurant we stopped at catered smoothly to my desire. The hot hamburger sandwich never varied down the coast to Los Angeles, east into Nevada, Arizona, north to Utah, Idaho, Montana, back through Wildhorse into Alberta. Slot machines and a hot hamburger; Boulder Dam and a hot hamburger; the Grand Canyon and a hot hamburger; the Mormon Tabernacle and a hot hamburger; Kalispell, a new bathing suit for my sister and a hot hamburger for me.

Why don't you try the fish and chips, my Mother pleaded, how about a club sandwich? Spaghetti and meatballs?

I could not be moved. I'll have a hot hamburger and a vanilla milkshake, please.

—◦—

Pat would cook it on his grill. Just a few steps around the counter, he'd serve you in one of the three booths looking out on Whyte Avenue. Pat washed dishes when things slowed down. He took your money when you left.

Certainly I loved Pat's hot hamburger sandwich in 1965. I had my own money in my wallet by then, and that was my own

Volkswagen Custom parked right out front. But by then my tastes were eclectic. By 1965 I would always read the menu. I might go for the pork chops, the veal cutlet. You couldn't lose at Pat's Lunch: everything came with two scoops of mashed potatoes, rich brown gravy, mixed veg., and two slices of tomato on a nest of lettuce.

I never saw Pat smile, not even when I paid the bill. Exactly what I wanted in a hole-in-the-wall cafe: a hot hamburger with mashed potatoes and no conversation. And what I wanted in a barber shop was just the haircut.

—◄o►—

So, what's your game?
Oh, I'm a graduate student.
Yeah? What in?
English.
English, bleh! My worst subject. Guess I'll hafta mind my grammar.

I'd love to have a dollar for all the times I've heard that. If he'd talked less and paid more attention to his work his comb might not have nicked open a pimple on my forehead. While he patched the hole with grey stuff that stung and turned black, he kept apologizing loudly in the crowded shop, running on and on about acne, funny how some get it and some don't! By the time he finished I felt like a freak on display—a low-class freak. The circus wouldn't even want me.

It was years later, it was 1980, before I got another barber like that, in Theo Bartels's—Kingston's Hairdresser to the Olympics. A barber was a hairdresser by then, and most were women. I should have known better. I should have scouted out one of those hole-in-the wall shops with a bored hairdresser lounging in her chair for a smoke, staring coldly at herself in the mirror. But sometimes the discipline slackens. I made an appointment at Theo Bartels's on the advice of a friend, the same friend who introduced me to Roy Kiyooka. Lose some and win some.

You wouldn't happen to have a nickname, wouldja, the hairdresser said to my dead pan in the mirror, like Old Stoneface or something? Oh, she was a kidder.

When are you going to start talking hairpiece, she asked, lifting my thinning bangs with her comb.

◂●▸

Sometimes it seems like I'm living it all mute and from the outside, like the green kid clad in the juices that ooze from trees. That's him now, frowning in at the second-storey window of the Darling nursery. The happy family scene within, which pen cannot describe, o'er which we must draw a veil, is not for him, not for me.

And yet I hauled my friend from Hong Kong along to Pat's Lunch.

Jam, this is Pat's Lunch, home of the best hot hamburger sandwich in Edmonton.

I've since become a tourist in Moosewood, The Horn of the Moon, The Enchanted Broccoli Forest, but I might still in the year 2003 select the hot hamburger sandwich or splurge on hamburger steak at the MOM (Mother's Own Method) Restaurant in Verona, Ontario. The MOM is run by Greeks who prepare a hot hamburger to the exact same North American folk recipe followed by Pat, and by Tony in the Star Cafe—Chinese-Canadian cuisine—in Oyen, Alberta. When I order a hot hamburger at the MOM, I'm not just slumming in my past.

Ah, but here I am, in Pat's Lunch, thirty-six years ago, where Pat has just plunked down our meals. Jam looks at her plate for a long time. I look at it too: the twin mounds of mashed potato, the tomato slices on the lettuce, the peas, diced carrots, and corn niblets, the patty smothered with gravy. Then she looks up at me with a guarded and serious expression on her face.

My expectant smile fades.

&

November 11, 1962. The ROTP cadets are marching in formation past the front of the Arts Building. It's the second month of my second year at the University of Alberta. I didn't plan to catch this parade, but I'm watching with interest when someone I've never met but admired from a distance strolls by. He's one of those suave undergraduates who always seems to know what's what, as I never do. He pauses beside someone standing near me & remarks, smirking to show that he isn't really inside what he says, Glorification of war? The acquaintance growls assent & they walk away together. I feel a flush of appalled resentment. Is that what with-it people think? I've been dragooned into attending Remembrance Day celebrations all my life & never heard a word of irony breathed about it, never a discouraging word. "In Flander's Fields" still holds all I know about the meaning of war.

In fourth year I joined the Canadian University Campaign Against Nuclear Disarmament. I subscribed to *Our Generation Against Nuclear War*. I was handing out anti-nuclear leaflets in the foyer of the Arts Building one time when a couple of passing rowdies taunted me. Chicken-shit, they sneered, scared of war! I was scared of *them*. I was afraid they'd grab my literature & tear it up. I couldn't understand what made them so angry with me. When they finally left, I was depressed. I hadn't been expecting ignorance, let alone hostility, & I'd acquitted myself badly. Now, to myself, I was arguing hotly, persuasively. I was converting them, changing them, though, I'm afraid, my tone was condescending. & what I really wanted to do was *punch them out*!

    I learned way more outside the classroom—introducing Jam Ismail to Pat's Lunch, now *there* was a lesson (culture & cuisine); shame it took decades to hit home—more outside than inside, until the classroom was my own. Then the balance began to right itself.

E

Rescue the Perishing

When my son Toby accepted Jesus Christ as his personal saviour he was in Grade Seven at Woodland Heights. He was born again in a bedroom on the second floor of the Berkshire Apartments on the corner of Springbank and Berkshire Drive. I didn't respond all that well to his announcement.

You *what*?

Not the right tone. I see that clearly now as I call the scene up. The excitement drained from his face. What he'd been eager to tell me would now have to be pulled out of him. He regretted having to show me his little New Testament and his Born Again certificate out of the Young Christian's Conversion Kit that his new school friend kept in his room. At least I should have apologized for shouting, since it was immediately too late to react as calmly as Penny had. Take it easy, she said, it's no big deal. She was right. She was often right, but not always, the proof being that she failed to notice what a fine human being I was evolving into. Not perceiving that, she left me.

In the School of Hard Knocks they don't necessarily beat you. I see this so clearly now. No, what they do is shock you, over and over, every time you step out on your own. Wrong! Wrong! Wrong! they shout, and you never learn to expect it. Of course it's always the one person shouting and shouting: Stupid! Stupid! Stupid! And that person is always your own father.

I had waited for Toby at the open door of that Christian apartment once, before he was born again. He hadn't had a close friend to go home after school with since Grade Three, so I was happy for him and I felt friendly towards his hosts. But none of them would look at me while Toby pulled on his boots—not his friend, not the little sister, not the mother. No one spoke to me, only to Toby. It has taken me all these years to be able to place myself in the kitchen of that apartment just after school, at the table where there is a glass of milk and a cookie apiece.

And what church do you go to, Toby?

I don't.

You don't go to church?

No.

Really!

◂o▸

At the Woodland Heights Science Fair Toby's project was titled The Fish of Ontario. We kept parts of that display for years. The pike and the bass and the walleye and the trout that I shaped out of styrofoam and Toby painted looked good hanging on the cottage wall. Walking between display rooms on the day of the fair we had met the junior missionary's mother, holding her daughter's hand. She didn't even glance at me; she couldn't stand to look at the vessel sinking beneath an innocent boy. I looked curiously at her, though, and what I saw was that her eyes *desired* my son. She desperately wanted to throw out a lifeline. I saw this through a smile so radiant I almost wished she would turn it on me.

In my religion, which I am improvising as I go along and keeping to myself, there is an Evil One tempting sons to leave their loving fathers who carve them fish and shout at them. There is an Evil One beguiling those sons, yea and the daughters also, to cleave to their True Father (which art in Heaven) and join Him in the Sweet Bye and Bye.

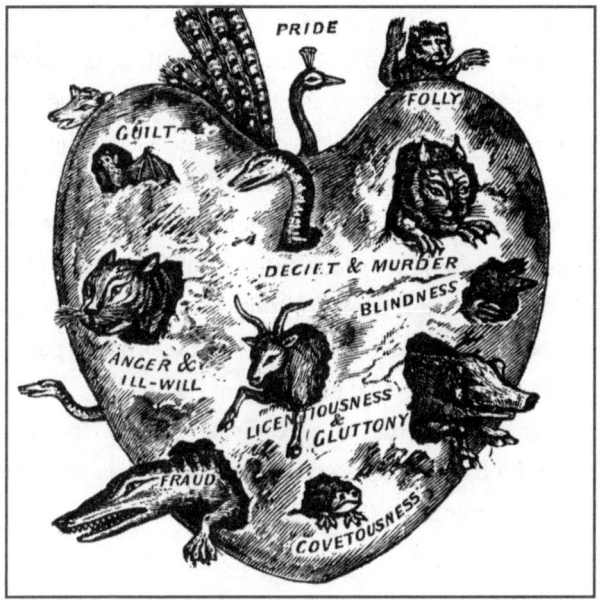

here is the creed of northern Icelanders as stated by the pastor in Halldór Laxness's *The Atom Station*: "[W]e believe in the land that God has given us; in the district where our people have lived for a thousand years; we believe in the function of country districts in the national life of Iceland; we believe in the green slope where Life lives." Whoa! Can this be a Lutheran pastor speaking? Ugla Falsdottir, the heroine, wonders too. "Oh yes, little girl," the pastor responds, "I believe in my God, we believe in our God. . . . It is certainly neither a Lutheran God, nor a Papal God; still less a Jesus God, although that happens to be the one most often named in the pastor's prescribed reading; neither is it Thor, Odin and Frey; nor even the stallion himself, as they think in the south. Our God is that which is left when all Gods have been listed and marked No, not him, not him." How could anyone not warm to a pastor who's half pagan & in thrall to no single system of names? Ugla wasn't sure she wanted her baby baptized in his Christian church. That's what got him talking. No problem. The ceremony may be held in the church, but "we shall dedicate her to the Slope of Life."

F

Police Will Not Turn Handle

I never prune my forsythia without talking to it: I know you want to thrive unchecked. I know you want your freedom to grapple for space with the Manitoba Maple, its powerful seed-keys parachuting into minute crack & crevasse, the subtle sumac suckering little periscopes all over the lawn. Fighting the plaintain, fighting the dandy lion. We didn't reckon with sumac imperialism, did we? Dug it out of a Nassagawaya meadow. Nassagawaya nugget, said my quondam brother-in-law, chuckling over a stone. The fields of that country are stone fields, he said, stone is what they grow. Dug it up and planted it out back. I know you want to duke it out between you, without the *unwanted designer trampling the woods*, the gardener with his garden shears.

    I have loved lawns ever since the time of all-day drives from Grimshaw in the Peace River Country Land of Twelve-Foot Davis down the dusty, slidy, gravel roads, sometimes gumbo roads in a downpour, sucking motion from the tires, five hundred miles south until bump! onto civilization—pavement—at Westlock, whirring on into Edmonton, Dad ostentatious, driving with one finger. Lawn after lawn, GREEN so GREEN and tidy, and I couldn't help but love the lawns and the white picket fences holding them in. What else would make me assume in later life (fairway, green) the game of golf? Mashie, niblick, cleek, putter, spoon. I hit a spoon shot on the seventh at Rivendell two summers ago that could not have been bettered. For once my mind left body alone and my heart leapt up to see the flight. Wilderness here, what's left of it, is a sand-trap. Hell Bunker. And I have a sand wedge in my bag.

Wild, wildness, wilderness, estrange, the other, outside. Yes, I want want want. Nature circulates its own—a bud, a shoot, antennae. That I want and lawn, even though, *Holy shit, Lawn grass,* mused the Stoned Horse in the suburbs of Universe City, *from that great tribe / they planted something to Mow.*

Did I show you my workshop? Did you see my banks of tiny compartment cases of screws, nails, wall fasteners, staples, cup hooks, washers, hinges, cotter pins, angle iron, tacks, all gear and tackle and trim, type upon type and once-upon-a-time all sized, and O if I'd only labelled the drawers, if only collection might have proceeded according to system. Alphabet, alphabet, why won't you stay at home?

what I learned from my 1980–81 graduate course, "Questions of Form in Contemporary Canadian Writing"—learned it the hard way in Hardknock U—was a better sense of what I could expect to fly in a class, what sort of text & what sort of approach. I don't know what I said that encouraged some students that year to write poems instead of essays for their seminar papers. I don't recall inviting response in kind to *The Martyrology*, for instance, but I was delighted when it happened & delighted when the assigned commentary on the paper turned out to be another poem. I was naively looking forward to the class in which all these layers of poem would be discussed.

    I didn't yet know that not all members of the class were similarly delighted. I wasn't hearing any of the grumbling about my course in the corridors of University College. I didn't know that students not enrolled in English 589 were referring to it as "Peyton Course." When I eventually heard that, I thought the wit misplaced, remembering *Peyton Place* as a steamy drugstore paperback passed around in high school decades before. "Is it up, Rod?" pants the high school slut, undulating her body under the body of the high school stud in the back seat of his car, "Is it up good & hard?"—a rhetorical question if ever there was one. "Oh, yes," he whispers, "Oh yes," & that's when she drives her knee up into his nuts. "Now go shove it into Allison MacKenzie," she screams. Unless there was more going on than I ever discovered, & I doubt it, the nickname for my class had nothing to do with sex. It must have been borrowed from the TV series based on the book, in which case *As the Course Turns* would have done just as well, because I'd apparently produced & was starring in a soap opera, either as hero or villain, depending on who you asked. I'm not a soap opera fan. Everything so fraught, the high emotion so continuous, cresting in little pre-commercial peaks—my irony drops me out. But I'd rather watch a soap opera than be in one. That was probably true of all the students in my class the day it blew up.

I don't think most students rebel unless there's something wrong. I don't *want* to be a shit-disturber, said one of the rebels in my office the day after the storm, & I believed her. Well, I believe her now, rehashing this painful episode in an otherwise gratifying teaching career, but at the time I was still recovering from the shock of finding out there was shit to disturb. The students who didn't understand *The Martyrology* wanted help rather than still more goddamn poetry. Okay, fair enough, but I was hurt by the assumption that I'd favour the "creative" rump, approval meaning higher grades. We took an extra hour to try to clear the air, & it helped the class to limp through the rest of the year, but twenty years later it still stirs up brown. I should have taken better care of the "conventional" students. I should have kept the conventional & the radical engaged like the teeth of gears.

I left teaching without having figured out for sure how to make a class work. Win some & lose some, that's all I can say about three decades of trying. I did manage better the next time I offered a course in difficult poetry. By then I was sensitized to discomfort, incomprehension, ready to acknowledge it respectfully & use it. First I acknowledged it in myself. "Poetry and Knowing," the course was called, but I said knowing is a verb, a process. Unknowing shadows it always. So let's try not to pretend we know more than we do—terrible impediment to learning. Worse yet is pluming ourselves on knowing more than somebody else.

Take me, I said. I've just picked up my twenty-five-year service pin, & after a quarter of a century what I know best is that I know very damn little. I'm often out of my depth, but I trust that some stranger—one of you, maybe; maybe myself—will pull me out before I drown.

The gamble worked. Nobody dropped the course on the grounds that I was a self-confessed ignoramus & I think I got some credit for trying to cut the distance between us. & this time the only person to offer a strange poem in response to a poem, at least in class, & not instead of literary criticism, was me.

"Police Will Not Turn Handle" is all that I kept of that "poem," my arrangement of all the odd fragments that came jumping out at me while I was reading Robin Blaser's *The Holy Forest*. I was mildly annoyed. Why no "useful" notes? Why am I thinking lawn? Why am I writing *Frankenstein*?

> There was a wrong man of spare parts, abandoned by his unnatural father, whose life was murder. Child, man, woman, he murdered what he loved. He was bad weather. There was a lightning at his birth, lightning and a blasted oak. Someone should have seen, someone should have known. Now we will never recover. Around the next corner, never, in the dark closet, never.

Why on earth *Pinocchio?*

> There was a wind, a vent,
> a ventriloquist and whether
> that was I or I was that
> wood-head with
> or without strings, Please
> I cried,
> I want to be real.

Where was all this coming from? From Blaser, some of it, yes, but there is something that wants more of me than I can understand. There was a *Holy Forest* disturbance. Something being stirred up. None of it brown.

The most difficult book on that course, the breaking point if there was going to be one, was Fred Wah's *Music at the Heart of Thinking*, which responds "drunkenly," improvisationally, to several other texts, including bpNichol's *The Martyrology*. Wah's writing is bunched, nonsensical, (im)personal, gone lurching its own road. & it is criticism. I file the book in the Ws of my poetry. Close enough. I can always find the book there & I seem to need it often, that & *Faking It: Poetics & Hybridity*. Both books help keep my thinking betwixt. They help keep certain questions a-boil: Is there a point at which the discipline of criticism lifts off the originating text & turns away into something else? How much will it stretch until—well, never; it never snaps in a reader of sufficient elasticity. How about the need for sharing discourse? Does it throw up certain limits?

 I was asking such questions in the course. I was treading that difficult ground again, but keeping everybody beside me now, one or two of them actually scared about not understanding, but saying so, talking to me, listening. For once I was balancing different degrees of aptitude & receptiveness. I was relaxed in my intensity. This equilibrium so fully engaged my physiology that by the time the course ended I was in near-perfect readiness for the game of golf, of which there is a zen well articulated by Will Smith as Bagger Vance in *The Legend of Bagger Vance*, a film not worth renting for any other reason.

G

The Columbia Icefields

It would have been a short jaunt off the Banff–Jasper highway to the edge of the Athabaska Glacier in 1942. Here is the post that marks the furthest edge of the ice in the year I was born. Somewhere in my mother's house there must still be a shoebox full of—what leaps into my head is not the glacier photos but the one of the smiling stranger with the hard-on, on the back of which my then twelve-year-old sister had written, "Notice anything funny?" There must be a box of photographs, snapshots, some of them tiny black-and-white views of the Columbia Icefields. There'd be a few loose shots of my dad. There was one of him that I particularly liked. He's on the move, wearing a snappy fedora and striding down Jasper Avenue in Edmonton, caught by one of those street photographers who snapped your picture and handed you a card with his number on it as you passed. But the unsorted photos are mainly of my mother's friends, her sisters. There are pictures taken at Mom's graduation from high school, from Calgary Normal School. In one she is smiling underneath a flowering trellis wearing 1930's slacks, in another she is teenaged with her father in his cloth cap and smoking his pipe, posed beside the Model T in the middle of a wheat field that rises to her chest. Some of these pictures are stories; some of them—my mother with old boyfriends—are possible futures. My mother alone? Not possible.

The future she chose, with my dad, begins in a series of photo albums. Silver photo corners licked and pasted on thick black paper. Here is the official wedding photo; here is me, newborn, in my mother's arms, in my dad's arms. In all of these pictures, before the series ends—my mother too busy, working full time—Dad is younger than I am now. It seems to me, looking at these early pictures, that he's afraid of dropping me. It looks like he'll hand me back to my mother as soon as the picture has been taken. It seems to me that, in a later photo, his arms encircle without holding my mother and her tenth-anniversary roses. I can tell by his eyes that he's not sober. It's clear enough now: the impatience with family life, the restlessness—seven years in Grimshaw was the longest stay in one place and one job—the hint of shadinesss. On the day when the north half of Grimshaw's main street burned down and my sister and I and the Stuart boys were kept home from school and Mom gave us cinnamon toast in the middle of the afternoon, my dad was one of the drinkers who kept track of the fire's progress from the hotel bar across the street until they remembered the lockers at the back of the butcher shop and a bunch of them rushed over to help carry out the frozen meat and in the confusion carried it right on home.

 The picture of the Icefields I'm thinking of was loose with all the others. A trip to the mountains with girlfriends, west off the bald prairie into the foothills, high up and into another country.

 In 1986 it's a long hike to the glacier's edge, walking past glacial rubble behind my sons who are racing to the ice. The field of ice is so brilliant from the highway and the souvenir shop below, so dirty-white up here. We're in our shirtsleeves because of the greedy sun. Be careful there—deep cracks in the ice. We will, they call back impatiently. But they're never careful enough, not so careful as I am, pointing my camera into these fantastically sculpted translucent blue crevasses alive with the deep-down chuckle of running water. I walked up here past markers of my life: my birth, my marriage, the births two years apart of these sons I'm so happy to be with high on this fabulous field of ice, my divorce.

The signposts with the years on them are getting further and further apart. I learned in Geography that glaciers are always on the move, and I learned how to recognize signs of the path of the mighty one that flowed from the Rockies out over the prairie—over all but the Cypress Hills—and over half a continent beyond, shaping esker, drumlin, moraine, scooping out shallow slough-beds, melting into Lake Agassiz, the vast ancestor of Lake Manitoba and the Great Lakes.

The Columbia Icefields are vast to walk on yet, or ride over in those yellow tourist buses with the massive tires, but look what a distance the ice has receded just between 1985 and 1986. I'm so happy to be up here with my boys, looking down at the glacier-cut valley lined with gravel, rock, boulders, then turning—a blink of the shutter—so sad to look up at the empty, abraded V between the peaks. Come with me now, our jackets off, the sleeves tied round our waists from the effort and the sun, stepping rock to rock way on up to the little crystal tarns, unfrozen—imagine!—for only two months of the year.

In the blue Canadian Rockies,
Spring is sighing through the trees
& the golden poppies are blooming
On the banks of Lake Louise.

H

Out-take

On the bus down to the optometrist on Richmond, just south of Dundas, I was reading Elizabeth Hay's first book. Dr. Bernardi had eyeballed my peripheral vision and thought it might not be what it should, so he arranged an appointment with this specialist who has a machine for testing peripheral vision.

For years before she died, my mother had nothing but peripheral vision. We had to admire the stubborn prairie will that kept her away from the eye-doctor, but she drove her Reliant at least five years longer than was safe. Is that a nickel or a dime, she'd ask, fingering her change to pay up at blackjack, and we'd joke (not seeing what should have been plain) that if she didn't know the difference, what was to keep us from robbing her blind?

My chin rested on one bracket and my forehead on another. I was wearing a pirate patch on one eye and holding a handle with a button on it to push whenever I saw a light that wasn't the one I was supposed to stare at. Honour system. That's your *Jeopardy* stick, the doctor said, and of course I couldn't resist asking what the prizes were. Ha ha. There was a loud clunk each time some star flashed in that gimcrack sky. Faint light? No light? I think I sometimes pressed the button at the sound cue, straining to beat the machine. Surely the doctor had picked it up at some high school science fair. But she seemed satisfied with it and she pronounced my peripheral vision okay. I didn't ask any questions; I wanted to get back to *Crossing the Snow Line:* "Yesterday in Toronto I argued with a producer. He said all artists tend to be conservative because they like form. I said form can be porous, liquid. Whatever dissolves."

Yes! A reader of your books needs to know this, Elizabeth Hay, and you saw that clearly enough to write it into the first one. You bind your words like an ancient Scots chariot: not solid like the more famous Roman model, but woven of willow withes. Strong to carry the weight but flexible, made to absorb the shocks of rough terrain.

That's my chariot too. I read these Elizabeth Hay books obsessively. It's like reading selves I could never imagine, but I recognize them instantly.

◄o►

"In a book like this," says Bobbie Louise Hawkins of her writing in *Almost Everything*, "the 'plot' is whether it can come together at all. It might help to think of it as having *gathered* more than having been written. It's got about as much plan to it as tumbleweeds blown against a fence and stuck there." I only saw those tumbleweeds once, driving through Saskatchewan on my first honeymoon, *our* honeymoon. Tumbleweed fences, drifts of tumbleweed high against the sides of barns and cowsheds. It was a dismal sight. But I'm all for the gathering, weed or flower, whatever just gathers before the sorting.

My (our) honeymoon, 1965. Portage and Main. North of Superior. The Plains of Abraham. The Halifax Citadel. Duckpins in Antigonish. Magnetic Hill. Green Gables. From Alberta to PEI and back in two weeks. Now that we aren't together I don't like pulling on the threads of those names, those memories snapped off like flower heads. Sometimes I do it, though, to move into strange country (losing my language) (not leaving home).

◀○▶

>How long's it been since we
>talked all night? God
>we used to be so close
>back then.
>
>>A fried egg sandwich
>>at 1:00 AM
>>on plain, white, store-bought bread.

That was the last song I could get to come together. It was before Penny and I split. It came out of Michael's breakup, which cost me his company every summer. He became the footloose one, loose from my life when his marriage shattered. The black summer before it finally happened I was shaking all over, shaking all over the surface, writing songs about family and home. I couldn't accept what was happening in the farmhouse down the road. I wouldn't dive into those currents, refused to see blood marks at the heart. I had put all wandering behind me and devoted myself to family. I thought my own devotion would be enough.

◀○▶

Turning and turning the new wedding ring in restaurants and cafes on the Trans-Canada Highway. Automatically pulling it off in that Dryden motel, leaving it on the dresser with the car keys where you saw it and hollered Hey! I looked where in mock dudgeon you were pointing, and we both broke up. I never got used to that ring. Finally you bought me another of flattened silver and I wore it comfortably for years, until it broke. I was doing without until the summer of my new resolve.

I bought the new ring on a trip to town, at Woolworth's in the Kingston Mall. Nicest ring I could get for $7.50. When we were up to speed on the way back, travelling north on the Sydenham Road, you in the rear and Michael beside me, I splayed my fingers on the wheel, I did left-hand contortions until I heard you gasp, then chuckle. Michael not knowing what was up, smiling at the warmth of the moment anyway.

—◁○▷—

So I thought my family was secure. Lonely at the cottage before the boys got out of school and you drove up with them, I wrote the family song that I've had to stop singing. Wrote it and sang it again and again that bad summer at the farm, blind to the pain I was causing every single time.

I really liked writing that song. My fingers were always finding things out about then. Knowing would switch off in my head and my fingers would feel out over the strings on their own. I had ways of using everything they found. A riff, a couple of chords, a melody—words for them always came. Word-love, home. I've stopped thinking I know anything. I'm so slow to understand these things. It was another ten years before I saw that Michael's separation tore me too, my words and music, apart. There were two more songs after "Fried Egg Sandwich," bits of song, chords and one or two verses. Then just half the form, the music. Then emigration. Home left me.

—◀o▶—

Inventory of My Bag (March 5, 1996):

wallet
five dollars Canadian
seven dollars American
ten rupees
credit cards
health card
library cards
membership cards
package of stamps
collected calling cards
chequebook
cheques
deposit slips
more credit cards
Canadian Tire card
address book
comb
lip balm
Tiger Balm
Extra Strength Tylenol
gluestick
nail clippers
extra car keys
extra cottage keys
savings account book

magnifying card
Swiss Army knife
pen
pen with golf club shirt-clip
Home Hardware pencil
compact flashlight
compass

Quite a self-portrait. Tumbleweeds caught against a fence? Whatever dissolves, whatever gathers? Don't you be fooled. This is Meccano. Girders and bolts. The whole secret superstructure thrown up and tightened into place so it will never fall down.

    A house for the rat-faced boy.

&

yes, I passed through a phase of trying to carry with me everything I might need in any possible situation. One degree more anal & I'd have listed all the functions of my Swiss Army knife. Tools—remarkable how much you can get into a small bag. "Pathetic," says Eeyore, looking at himself in the water of the stream on the day of his birthday, and so say I. Pathetic. Your life shatters & you figure to gain control with a gadget bag, a utility belt? I spent the year after my marriage broke up on sabbatical, trying to write in a carrel in Western's library. Every day I walked to a different place in the stacks & picked a book out at random, photocopied the title page & pasted it into a scrapbook. Why? I get these temporary urges to collect things together, get them sensibly arranged. That was about all I accomplished that bad year—a random collection of title pages from other people's books.

But I like making inventories. Every summer for years I made a list of everything I took with me first time to my writing tent. To kick off another summer I hoped would be a good one for writing and for living. Those inventories were really invocations, displaced scraps of a form & a tradition I loved & couldn't live in.

It's unfair to mention a rat-faced boy out of a novel-in-slow-progress. In the novel he has a name, Silas, though most of his acquaintances call him deef & dumb. Or idiot. Rural eastern Ontario in the first decade of the twentieth century was no place to be deaf & mute. The rat-faced boy is a character I begin to see that I can love. Good thing, because though I'm inventing him I dimly see from what.

Bobs Yer Uncle

"Jesus, Dorf," Karen said, "don't say <u>thus</u>."
Robert Kroetsch

January 13, 1997
Dear Bob,

    A funny thing happened on the way to this sentence. I was downstairs looking for *Silence*—John Cage, you understand—but *Silence* was neither with the downstairs criticism nor with the downstairs poetry, and I had just remembered where I saw it last, in an upstairs bookcase crammed with decades of complimentary Norton anthologies—repudiating the whole Norton enterprise—when I was waylaid by Charles Bernstein. I need *Silence* for tomorrow's class. My student Kevin Davis has written a strange triptych for Steve McCaffery and I want to read him something supportive, and I have to mark two essays for Wednesday, today being Monday but Tuesday is full, and I haven't got time to open *Content's Dream* and run my finger down the Contents. Bob, I haven't got time to flip to Bernstein's Introduction to Robin Blaser. I mean it, Bob, if Bernstein's piece on Blaser hadn't been just two pages long, I wouldn't have had a snowball's chance in hell of making it here.

◄o►

> IF THERE WERE A PART OF LIFE DARK ENOUGH TO KEEP OUT OF IT A LIGHT FROM ART, I WOULD WANT TO BE IN THAT DARKNESS, FUMBLING AROUND IF NECESSARY, BUT ALIVE   AND I RATHER THINK THAT CONTEMPORARY MUSIC WOULD BE THERE IN THE DARK TOO, BUMPING INTO THINGS, KNOCKING OTHERS OVER AND IN GENERAL ADDING TO THE DISORDER THAT CHARACTERIZES LIFE (IF IT IS OPPOSED TO ART) RATHER THAN ADDING TO THE ORDER AND STABILIZED TRUTH AND POWER THAT CHARACTERIZE A MASTERPIECE (IF IT IS OPPOSED TO LIFE)   AND IS IT?   YES IT IS.

February 13, 1997
Dear Bob,

Her breasts—is it more tender to mention them individually than as a pair?—they were *way* out there. Head-on or profile, you'd have to be blind to miss them. Though of course the blind have their braille. *I* didn't miss them, indeed no, but I don't think I telegraphed. I did wonder about her workplace, though. I worried about her fellow workers talking behind her back.

But people would *have* to talk behind the back of a front like that.

Wouldn't they?

Not a contemporary set, somehow. Somehow gathered and launched as for maximum thrust. Nature or art? I think that's still a good question.

I just had to wonder, Bob, and I thought I'd tell you. Some of these old subjects will be lost completely if some of us old subjects don't keep wondering them through. Maybe we could sit down together some time and just wonder back and forth reverently, without any smirking or nudging. We could ask ourselves, does adolescence ever end or does it only kind of ripen?

I *don't* have just one thing on my mind, Bob—that's the trouble—and neither do you.

March 13, 1997
Dear Bob,

It was late Friday evening before I realized I'd left my briefcase on the bus to your place. On Monday you retrieved it from the Winnipeg Transit Lost and Found, somewhere beneath downtown Winnipeg. Retrieved the briefcase and sent it to me in London, Ontario. Notes from a week of research at the Hudson's Bay Archives. Having put you to the trouble, I was glad at least that the rescue involved an underground journey. And in your living room that Friday evening you told me you thought I was acquainted with silence.

My sister has said almost the same thing, using different words. Driving to London from the 1985 family reunion in Lacrosse, Wisconsin, she eventually asked from the back seat, my mother in the front, Why don't you say something, for godsake?

If you'd shut up for fifteen seconds, I snapped, I might be able to!

For the first hundred miles of a prattle remarkable for the complete absence of shadow between thought and (continuous) speech, I thought of *The Clockmaker*: "A woman's tongue goes so slick of itself, without water power or steam, and moves so easy on its hinges, that it's no easy matter to put a spring stop on it, I tell you." For the next hundred miles I thought of Jack Lemmon in *Under the Yum Yum Tree*: "Merciful Heavens, will there *ever* be a respite!" Finally, I was just going nuts, thinking shut up, shut up, shut up, until the question surprised me into speech.

If she *had* paused, of course, I wouldn't have spoken. I like driving, and I like driving silent so my pinball thoughts may carom as they will. So there I was, revealed to my salt-of-the-earth sister as the sour solitary shit that I am.

> There's a poplar tree
> waiting for me
> out where the prairie rolls
> (Don't the prairie roll)
> and the beauty of that place
> is that the whole human race
> is just me.

Yes, but if you've flown all the way to Winnipeg to read for a week in the Hudson's Bay Archives and have then arrived at the house of a friend, with suitcase but without briefcase, would it not be appropriate once in a while to open your mouth, whether in discourse large or small? For that friend to mark the long silences and then dignify his tongue-tied visitor with the acquaintance of silence itself—

Of course you do have to hand it to my sister, Bob, and here's just one of the reasons why: we were at Ontario Place in 1977, Penny and the kids and me showing Toronto to the aunt from Alberta. It was Betty's first trip east. Manfred couldn't leave the dairy, but he could spare Betty for a while, even if it *would* be awfully quiet without her. We were in the Imax Theatre, viewing a multi-image presentation on Ontario arts and crafts. There was too much for any one pair of eyes to absorb, so I would never have known, had Betty not picked it out, that some Ontario artist had made a briefcase out of the rear end of a cow and left the asshole in. She saw that rear view every day of her life, though without the handles, and I guess it just jumped out at her.

So, says Marnie, after I read her the foregoing,

> the asshole of a briefcase
> and the briefcase of an asshole:

is that what you're going for?

What a critique, Bob! As you know, effective use of chiasmus can be devastating.

April 13, 1997
Dear Bob,

In Buffalo this spring, the evening before the Louis Zukofsky Conference that Robert Creeley organized, I was listening to a Canadian and her South African partner wonder how to talk about their countries to the Americans they live among. Try this for Canada, I said. This is Robert Kroetsch: "It may be that we survive by being skilful shape-changers. But more to the point, we survive by working with a low level of self-definition and national definition. We insist on staying multiple, and by that strategy we accommodate to our climate, our economic situation, and our neighbours." Well, I paraphrased, but I do keep most of that in my head. I like to offer it to my classes, saying, here you are, here's the Canadian identity you don't think you can find. If I had been elaborating in Buffalo (but I never do) I might have said tell your American friends to look for us Canadians in the Strait of Anian.

The where?

The Strait of Anian. The Northwest Passage. Still devilish hard to find. Tell them to read George Bowering's *Burning Water*.

"It may be that we survive . . . " I think it's necessary to be full of something to create such a we. Not what you think. Extravagance. I love that *we*, Bob. I have stood under it. Your *we* and *our* and *us*. Opening *The Lovely Treachery of Words* at (no kidding) random, here's another: "It is Nichol who teaches us a Miltonic scorn for economy." Why is it that perversely I start to resist *we* now? Without *we* there is no theory. There is no community.

Having been at the party that inspired Michael Ondaatje's poem, "Claude Glass," having been one of the drunks at that party—but drunk only to the point of extravagance, drunk merely to the exercise of contortional dancing and violent non sequitur—I see where the poem breaks from the real party. In the poem, for example, about 4 AM the morning after, a late guest arrives:

> The invited river flows through the house
> into the kitchen up
> stairs, he awakens and moves within it.

Well, the house was bone-dry when I got back there the next afternoon. *All through the night,* Depot Creek had quietly kept within its banks. But only a fool prefers fact over full fathom five. I marvel at the sea-change of the poem. It is and is not the same party I partied. I should know better than to keep wondering who was the "unhappy shadow" at the party on the page,

> That friend who said he would find
> the darkest place, and then wave.

Was there an original for this black vortex of repudiation the drunken speaker keeps revolving round? The likeliest one was apparently passed out with his head in his arms on the kitchen table until the fiddle came out and broke into "Smash the Windows." He opened his eyes and made a quizzical remark which the fiddler fiddled back at him. He grinned and stood up. He pushed the chair back to give his legs room. A new wave of the party was rising. Not him, then, so who was that unhappy shadow?

It certainly wasn't me. I was the guitar.

Why keep worrying this point when I no longer need to? Having followed John Thompson through *Stilt Jack* to this:

> If one more damn fool talks to me about
> sweetness and light . . .
>
> I'm looking for the darkest place;
> then, only then, I'll raise my arm. . . .

Opening wide the gap between myself and an opinion I share, I seem to be opting out, standing aside, writing myself into that darkest place. Leaving the party. There is something out there I need. Out there in the field below stars, standing on a chunk of Shield, looking back at the lights of the house.

Wendy, John, and Michael slip out of their beds and hurry to their mother, who cannot believe her eyes. Can these be her innocent and heartless children, returned after so many desolate nights of watching? There is a thrill to Mrs. Darling's voice as she calls George out of the dog-house, and Nana the hairy nursemaid rushes to join the happy scene in the nursery, and this is how Peter Pan, that little green dog-in-the-manger, sourly witnesses the Darling family reunion: "He had ecstacies innumerable that other children can never know; but he was looking through the window at the one joy from which he must be forever barred." The best Peter can do out there is exchange jaggy remarks with that fool, his narrator. Why should *he* feel left out?

That dark waver wasn't looking for company. He *meant* to absent himself from felicity. The last thing he wanted was a party. He got invited anyway. It makes no difference how dark and silent the place you retreat to; if it's pure enough, someone will be drawn to you. One, two, many: another *we*, a fester of solitaries, a community of outsiders.

> For certain engineering purposes, it is desirable to have as silent a situation as possible. Such a room is called an anechoic chamber, its six walls made of special material, a room without echoes. I entered one at Harvard University several years ago and heard two sounds, one high and one low. When I described them to the engineer in charge, he informed me that the high one was my nervous system in operation, the low one my blood in circulation. Until I die there will be sounds. And they will continue following my death. One need not fear about the future of music.

May 13, 1997
Dear Bob,

"There are times when I see at the core of his writing a tall, gangly, full-frontal-naked, symbolic prick. Something is making him shamefaced. It must be the ruby glow of his erect penis, the prick of this prick. What's he done, gone and scalded it again?" So I wrote, about that maypole, flagpole, newel post, that homuncular gopher, grain elevator, Calgary Tower, UP and singing out of each of your books: *I am calling you ou-ou-ou, ou-ou-ou.* Never re-read what you write, Bob. I'm saying this to myself. Never take yourself out of context. Having done so, I sound prissy. I sound like a man who has never heard the call, never cocked an ear to the imperious trill of the flighted phallus.

No. No prick, but a happy unhappiness, a suffering insufferable denying desiring. Not at the core, not at the edge. Dissolve these terms. Or shuttle between them. You didn't get it into words. If you had found words for it, *this* poor suffering insufferable indivisible as-is would not have understood your standing under and reaching. Reaching, desiring. I don't get it. I want it. You don't give it to me. All along that body arching *in extremis* throbs an unsatisfied mind.

>
> You did let it hang out, Bob,
> and you wrung your technic like a rag,
> why I return to you
> > lonesome
> again and again.

June 13, 1997
Dear Bob,

Love,

Stan

&

(As told to Vaclav and Vera Slavik, Czech translation by Ivo Moravec, on June 20, 1997.)

I was at a conference on the weekend, in Waterloo. It was called the Robert Kroetsch Celebration. We were honouring one of our most important writers on his seventieth birthday.

> *Víkend jsem strávil na konferenci ve Waterloo. Nazývala se "Pocta Robertu Kroetschovi." Oslavovali jsme sedmdesáté narozeniny jednoho z našich nejdůležitějších spisovatelů.*

I read my contribution on Friday. I was reading along in the first part of it when I came to an extra page. Two pages with the same thing on them.

> *Přednesl jsem svůj příspěvek v pátek. Při čtení úvodní části jsem narazil na jednu přebytečnou stránku. Dvě stránky s identickým textem.*

So I pulled out one of the two & put it aside and said to the audience that it was extra & anyone who liked could have it.

> *Odložil jsem jednu z nich stranou s poznámkou, že je navíc a kdokoliv z publika má zájem, může ji mít.*

Then I was reading a little further along & I came to a line about pruning my forsythia—not that it matters what it was about—& I turned the page and . . . whoops! Some lines were missing.

> *Pokračoval jsem ve čtení až k řádku o prořezávání mé*

*forsythie—ne že by záleželo na tom, o čem to bylo—
otočím stránku a ... jejda! Několik řádků se ztratilo.*

There wasn't much missing, but it was enough to stop me, enough that I couldn't improvise a bridge. So I had to say why I'd stopped & then eventually just start up where I left off.

Nescházelo jich mnoho, ale přesto dost na to, aby mne zarazily, dost na to abych je nemohl překlenout improvisací. Musel jsem přiznat proč jsem zmlkl a nakonec znovu začít tam, kde jsem se přerušil.

This kind of thing is everybody's nightmare, isn't it? Being in public, up on stage, & things start to go wrong. Things go completely out of your control.

Něco takového musí být pro každého noční můra. Být na veřejnosti, stát na jevišti a věci se začnou sypat pod rukama. Věci se kompletně vymknou kontrole.

People who were due to speak on Saturday told me they rushed back to their rooms after my session & checked to see that they had all their pages, & in the proper order.

Lidé, co měli hovořit až v sobotu, mi říkali, že jakmile jsem skončil, uháněli do svých pokojů aby se ujistili, že oni mají stránky všechny a v náležitém pořadí.

So I was reading the second part of my presentation. This was the one that meant the most to me, because it was addressed to Robert Kroetsch. I had written it for this day.

A tak jsem četl druhou část svého příspěvku, část, která pro mne znamenala nejvíce, protože byla adreso-

> vaná Robertovi Kroetschovi. Napsal jsem ji právě pro tento den.

It went along fine until I got to the second-last piece—I was reading a series of Dear Bobs, open letters to Robert Kroetsch—& the second-last letter was missing. Gone.

> Četl jsem ze seriálu otevřených dopisů nazvaných "Milý Roberte" a čtení probíhalo hladce až k předposlednímu dopisu. Předposlední list chyběl. Zmizel.

& this was the one I'd most wanted to read. It had the real stuff in it that I wanted to say about Bob Kroetsch's writing. It had my heart in it.

> A byl to ten, který jsem chtěl číst nejvíce ze všech. Obsahoval to nejpodstatnější co jsem chtěl o psaní Roberta Kroetsche říci. Mluvil mi z duše.

But I'd had enough of glitches by this time. I just read on to the last piece & thanked the audience & they applauded & I went to my seat.

> To už jsem měl malérů dost. Pokračoval jsem posledním listem, poděkoval obecenstvu, oni zatleskali a já se usadil zpět na svém sedadle.

& I sat there while the chair of the session got up to thank everyone, wondering where in hell that second-last piece had got to & riffling through my pages &, for godsake, I found it!

> Zatímco předsedající konference kráčel k mikrofonu aby všem poděkoval, vrtalo mi hlavou kam se ten zatracený předposlední list mohl podít. Jak jsem se probíral těmi svými stránkami, prokristapána, já ho našel!

I don't know if it had stuck to the previous page or what, but now that I was finished, there it was.

> Nevím, jestli se přilepil k předchozí stránce nebo co, ale ted', když jsem skončil, já ho mám.

I'm not suave in these situations, you know, not suave at all, but for some reason I didn't hesitate. I said, "Just a minute, Gary." This was to the chair of the session, who had begun to thank me. "Just a minute," I said, "I have another piece to read."

> Nebývám zrovna důsledný v těchto situacích, znáte to, nebývám vůbec důsledný, ale z nějakého důvodu jsem nezaváhal. Řekl jsem: "Okamžik, Gary. Chci přečíst ještě jeden list."

& I got up and read it, but first I said, "I can't believe I have the gall to do this."

> Vstal jsem a přednesl ho, napřed jsem ale řekl: "To by mě zajímalo, kde se ve mně tahle nestydatost bere."

In a group of strangers there's no way I *could* have done it, but even though there were a lot of people I hadn't met in that audience, they *were* my family & Bob really was our uncle.

> Kdybych byl mezi cizími, v žádném případě bych to nemohl udělat, ale i když v obecenstvu bylo hodně lidí s nimiž jsem se ještě nesetkal, byli moje rodina a Bob byl ve skutečnosti náš strejček.

What I didn't say was that my letters were called "Bobs Yer Uncle," which is . . . which is hard to explain, at least the way it's normally used. It's a . . . what? An idiomatic phrase. Well, never mind that.

> *Co jsem ale neřekl, bylo, že jsem svým dopisům říkal 'Strejček na kompletního Boba', což jest . . . to se těžko vysvětluje . . . aspoň v normálním významu. Je to . . . co? Úsloví. No co, nechme to plavat.*

Anyway, I read the second-last piece last & sat down for good.

> *Zkrátka a dobře, přečetl jsem předposlední list jako poslední a definitivně se posadil.*

&, you know, some people actually came up to me afterward & asked if I'd staged the whole thing. Apparently they'd liked the mistakes.

> *A věřili byste tomu, že někteří lidé ke mně potom chodili a vyptávali se, zda jsem to měl všechno nacvičené? Zjevně se jim ty chyby zalíbily.*

Win some and lose some, eh?

> *Vítězství a prohry, eh?*

Makes you wonder.

> *Podivu hodné.*

Mr. Slavik had French & German, but no English. Any Canadian should know French, & not just because the government says so. I told Mr. Slavik that, through Ivo, apologizing for my unilingual status. He had been a member of the Czech government & then a persecuted dissident. He had good reason to feel ironic about government. I would have felt his integrity across the gulf of language even if I hadn't known about his resistance to Czech totalitarianism & his approval of Ivo's defection with Jana & young Ivo. Ivo would never boast about his father, nor about himself, but I knew their story because Ivo had written it in a book called *Tightrope Passage*. It would be a long story to tell how that book of escapes was lived & how it got written & published in Canada. I played a small part in bringing author to publisher. For this, for my having merely had the good sense to recognize a wonderful & unusual book, Ivo was unreasonably grateful, & so were his parents. That was something else I could feel, though nothing was said about it.

Before Ivo's English translations, I could hear much in his father's Czech. I heard stylish intelligence, wit. I heard much in his Czech rhythms that drew me to the man. He didn't think he was coming across, though. I sensed his frustration. But, after all, how much language do we really need? Just before Mr. Slavik stepped out the door at the end of the evening, he looked at me & placed his hand on his heart. I did the same, to show that I understood. Where was the distance between us then?

I wish we had been able to talk freely, Mr. Slavik & I, even if his single gesture said everything, but I loved telling my story with pauses for translation. I have a deep & unreasonable resistance to speech, a near-paralyzing reticence. I want to be anywhere but on stage, even though the stage is my own living room. All my anecdotes fail. I tell them too spasmodically or I forget something important or I stop too abruptly. People are always asking, after a polite pause, That's it? That's the story? So here is my resolution: always to speak with my translator by my side. You may think you understand my language. Never mind. You have to wait until Ivo finishes. Ivo's translation is my refrain. During the refrain I am gathering myself for the verse. In the verse you hear me saying *exactly* what I mean to say, & you hear me setting my meaning into such perfect rhythmic motion that it glides through the porches of your ears & zings into the cockles, the *sanctum sanctorum* of that compromised seat of wisdom your mind.

J

"If you can't say something nice,

don't say anything at all." My mother had a lot of that sort of commonplace wisdom at her fingertips. "More haste, less speed" was another. She would have needed the latter less often if she hadn't married Dad and had kids. I can almost hear her hissing it grimly to herself while she bustles around inside the Grimshaw house, taking care of last-minute stuff before we can leave on vacation. Because Dad is sitting out in the car with us kids, and has been for fifteen minutes, "champing at the bit" in our horseless carriage, the cream-coloured Studebaker. Betty is four, Stanley is six, Kenneth is thirty-seven. We're all of one mind: "Let's go, let's *go!*"

"If you can't say something nice . . ." Mom lived by that one. She had a fierce, democratic tolerance. A person was always a person to her. With absolutely no reluctance, she devoted hours of extra instruction to the duller kids in her classes. I never heard her bad-mouth anybody, not even Dad, not even after we all grew up and moved away and she finally regained her blessèd independence by divorcing him. Him and his restlessness, his inability to settle, to hang on to a job. "Handsome is as handsome does," right? I'm beginning to wonder if I absorbed a way of hanging fire on my opinions because of the total congruence between word withheld and judgment suspended in my mother. What she never taught, but lived before me all the years of her life.

But this isn't an encomium. Sometimes I've wanted strong

opinions and wanted them *right now.* Sometimes I've found myself hesitating when it would have been right, and I knew right then it was right, to say, to *shout* Yes! or No! and I've gritted my teeth on the word and walked away with a sinking opinion of myself. Once more in the destructive element immerse, dear friends. I heard, I hesitated, the moment was gone.

&

May 1995, on the train back from Montreal, reading Erin Mouré's *Search Procedures* with such delight that words of my own are freed "as if layered in the head, words linked by dint of/ 'interpretation,' each layer oscillating, ignites cortical screens or paths/ unavailable to the expulsive reader who dismisses 'absolute' a piece/ where so little 'actually' fits together, there is no palpable image or whole/ or the 'whole' is an elaborate leap of memory, of inner voice &/ melody . . ."

Kispiox. Brudenelle. Flower of Scotland.

Search Procedures is full of strong opinions, some of them in footnotes, pugnacious & disarming. This one hilariously preempts, parodies, the hostile critic:

> We are now completely off the subject of New Jersey. The author has failed in her task. The electricity bills due to lighting are interminably high & for what effect; for all her talking, we still have not overcome "the scorched earth policy." She's fired! There is an opening for a real poet in these pages.

& I'm loving these metonymic anti-referential new-sentence abnormal flight *procedures* laying wide the poetic field, down & acrossward, clambering up the, like, beanstock. I added that, the new free fields & the Giant Hall above the clouds, with new commonplaces, as e.g., small "deer." See, it's happening again—

> carrying the letter "a"
> which she loves, in the alphabet,
> which is "lovable,"
> which she also loves.

I'm such a long aloft from home. My mother never told me. "There is more space over a cat than under & the birds are hogging it." Such a long, but curiously too at home with the language so leaping demo, cratic, the compo-zition zinging. How are you saying zed? I'm not feeling at all expulsive, until suddenly . . .

& there I had to leave the writing to catch up with the (*extreme* cortical spendour) re-reading. It was not my intention to get carried away.

Ah, "intention."

Later. Do I feel foolish! Good thing I didn't finish that sentence, because "suddenly" has no place here. The slight to Roo Borson I remembered is nowhere in *Search Procedures.* In the re-reading it did not suddenly appear. But everything in this & was heading towards it! An earlier draft had a strophe of appeal—greater tolerance between writers, more elasticity of taste. So what was it that put my back up? Could it have been once overhearing Bronwen Wallace say that Erin Mouré had called her an obsolete realist, a nineteenth-century poet? How to square that remark with the existence of a book of correspondence between Wallace and Mouré?

Read the book: *Two Women Talking: Correspondence 1985–87.* In this collection of exchanges under the aegis of the Feminist Caucus of the League of Canadian Poets, Erin Mouré patiently tries to encourage Bronwen Wallace to think more theoretically, specifically about language itself as a problem for women. She sends Bronwen a number of *Tessera* essays & long letters discussing the language issues in them. The pressure turns Bronwen defensive. I don't see evidence for it, but she thinks her aesthetic & her writing, even her experience as a woman, is under attack. She first tries & then turns away from engaging the notion that *language itself subordinates the feminine.* True, Erin pushes hard. In a footnote to her last letter to Bronwen, she actually suggests that Bronwen might begin

> by stating that <u>one effect</u> on writers who agree with

people like [Xavière] Gauthier and [Dale] Spender <u>has been</u> (*the underlined emphasis is to be careful not to accuse anyone of having a monolithic viewpoint, which a) would be projecting an impression of yours onto them, and b) would polarize (which, as we see, closes argument))* a rejection of the narrative line, saying that is an attempt to mirror or represent reality, and language cannot represent (purely) the world. Then open your perspective on story (don't discount theirs! Just show your slide on the screen at the same time), that in the telling, you are looking for that hidden something behind the story (a power, a kind of grave, a force, mental connection, synaptic leap . . .), using those neural connections of straight story to break through and make new connections. This is NOT representation, but something else, then. *Bronwen, what is it? Think about and articulate this! Go ahead! I double dare you!"*

It doesn't seem that Bronwen did, not at the 1987 panel on women and language. It doesn't seem as though Bronwen was ever persuaded to respond in the terms presented, not if the remark I overheard in 1988 is any indication.

Bronwen, what is it? Maybe it seemed to Bronwen that Erin knew *what it is* & just wanted Bronwen to catch on, catch up. After all, Erin had presented Bronwen with the bones of a possible Wallace argument that might bridge the gap between them, or at least spark across it. On one level, not one Bronwen would be proud to be stung by, this might have read *I can think your own thoughts better than you can. My mind has more bite.* More? Different. I hear Erin wanting to stretch Bronwen, yes, & perhaps through a revelation that has already astounded her, but the invitation is into a process. Bronwen died, so she couldn't continue, either to change or resist, & so Erin gets the last word, which comes first in the pamphlet, in the Foreword:

> What's tricky is that we're only capable of listening out of our own world view, the mind attends only to what it can recognize, and the process of recognition is one of elimination, in which the mind ignores what does not make sense to it, literally creates gaps that are invisible and seamless. So any two people, in such a discussion, operate over invisible and seamless gaps, but this is THE WAY IT IS, at the boundary when we have clambered over the scrap heap of "what we know," and proceed forward, into what we don't, into what we are not sure of, into what is incomplete and bothering us. And one can never think forward, add to one's capabilities of thinking, language, text, world . . . without coming up against the challenge of someone else's thought.

Bronwen, what is it? I feel the heat of intellectual curiosity in that. Or is it extra-intellectual, that drive to find out how to find out more than we know? That's in fact in what Bronwen wrote in a statement she declined to have printed in the 1987 feminist caucus program ("I never know what the poem will discover"), but, in the same sentence, is a retreat to familiar ground ("but for me, that everyday language is a sort of safety net, a familiar place in which a deeper, often more dangerous exploration can take place").

I think Bronwen thought she was losing this exchange. I think Erin wanted to get past polarization, beyond winning & losing. But it does look to me as though her intelligence will focus more finely, as an acetylene torch becomes too bright for the unprotected eye & then cuts steel. She's too good a student not to be a teacher. If I walk to her side, & I do, I take Bronwen with me. Together we'll find a way to uncircle the wagons. Those people are riding around and whooping out there because Universal Studios told them to. We don't understand them yet, but they aren't the enemy.

Yes, & here's my friend Phil Hall (Bronwen's friend also, & Erin's friend) bestriding the same dilemma: how to speak in language broken & tormented into such new shapes that the audience of plain people he wants most—this is the risk—least wants him. His solution is to accept himself as a "Mandelstam in Guthrie Clothing." He let the wolf in at the door, you see, & there ensued a merry chase. & now whose bright, breaking falsetto ("Come in, dearie!") rings out behind the door? & is that really Granny with the covers up to her chin? That's Granny's nightcap; I'd know that nightcap anywhere.

It may not be Phil's fate to be devoured, but he knows that relinquishing shared language has a cost:

> Dreaming at lucid dawn I hear (last month) an internal critic refer to me as "Mandelstam in Guthrie clothing." (Osip, of course; Woody, of course—my durable unlikely godparents.) I see what that inner-critic means:
>
> I am becoming more hermetic and more populist at the same time!
>
> It's true: ask me to read my poems and—*as a defense, as a persona, as late aspiration, as a pretense of connection with my origins*—I pull on my slouch-cap; I get out my songs, harmonica and confessions (confusions).
>
> But let insomnia have me (or the anonymity of travel, or the isolation of illness, or . . .) And I'm parsing, coining joint-words, genuflecting to Polish literature, revising poems in copies of my old books, finding otherhood in the cryptics of Paul Celan.

So Phil says in *The Unsaid*, & the title of his next book is illustrative: *Hearthedral: A Folk-Hermetic*.

& if you'd heard Phil "read" at the Eastern Edge Gallery in St. John's on April 28, 2001, you'd have cheered—if with all your heart you wanted the Guthrie-Mandelstam and all such binaries dissolved, fresh & compatible & acceptable to all—you'd have goddamn well cheered as Phil wrapped the Hall hermetic in talk & tucked it in between stanzas of an old Ontario folk ballad. There he was whole: functional, accessible, familial, spellbinding. Phil Hall, true friend to very different people—complete strangers, some of them. Stranger families.

What I meant to say: my mother didn't teach me the propulsive value of irritation.

K

For Crying Out Loud

Somebody should at least have helped me to find a proper seat. That might've been the key right there. It *might've*. I don't know. Maybe I'm trying to duck something. Okay, I *am* ducking. Okay, I'll *get* to it. Still, all it would have taken was one person who knows something, and god knows there were enough of those around. Gerry, for one. Sure, he stands up when he plays, but even he must have been a novice once. Gerry's not that sensitive, but he might've taken a look out from behind the sound console, a look out at the fifty-year-old guitar player searching for a seat that wouldn't collapse out from underneath him like the one he found did three-quarters of the way through the longest night of his life. A little, three-cornered crippled gimcrack drummer's stool tossed in the back room of the gallery after some medieval gig of the Nihilist Spasm Band—each of whose members would've *liked* the fucking chair dropping one, two, many times out from under. It's in their mandate. So I found the rickety metal stool and brought it out and set it up. Why not a chair? Chair wouldn't look right? Look right! *Think* right. Trying to adjust my ass-level to get the guitar at mike level, now that's low-quality thinking. Half a brain could tell you not to start at the ass. I see that now. Sure, it could've been worse. But it wasn't "moving right along" to have so much trouble getting the stool to stand up under my ass again and stay there after it fell out. It came to this: I had no confidence in my seat. If it hadn't been for worrying about that seat I wouldn't have forgotten the words to "Zucchini Tragedy." Sure, I forgot the words playing it for Fraser and Debolt, but that was different. Daisy wanted Ray to hear it down in the basement of that coffee house in Hamilton between their sets. I seized up right after "kiss my zucchini ass." *Real* musicians are cool. They go to hear other musicians play and between sets they all gather backstage or in the basement or in the green room and everybody plays their latest and everybody feels good about the art that's going on, you know, creative mind feeding creative mind until the beauty that breaks from thee then is just sickening. *Real* musicians never forget the words to their own songs. It isn't done. So. I forgot my words that one other time and if it hadn't been for that lapse I'd be on the folk festival circuit right now and "Zucchini Tragedy" would be known and loved from sea to sea to sea. Yes, and I'd be killing myself another way than this. The truth is, I wouldn't have forgotten the words if my left hand hadn't suddenly let me down. After a million times through the one song you should be able to trust your left hand on its own. We're not talking complicated here, but there's a point in every verse where the F chord slides up three frets, tum-tum-tum, a fret at a time. *Real* musicians bar the E chord up—musicians like I would have been but for that lapse in the basement of the Hamilton coffee house—but as for me and my house, son, we slide with the F. And when the time came for the slide that night, my hand just didn't bother. It didn't quit; it kept on playing, but ... other chords. If my brain's whole wiring hadn't been needed for the red alert I might've tried pleading. Don't desert me, Bully. Work with me, man. It seemed a long, long way out there, all the way down the left arm to the hand. What with the fingers going their own way and the stool threatening to fall out from under my ass any minute—it's easy to see from here: of *COURSE* I'm going to forget the words.

Okay, o*kay*. It happened one other time before the Hamilton time, at the Yardbird Suite in Edmonton, and now we've been through my entire performing history, except in England, but I was drunk there every time and, anyway, the folk tradition props you up so you believe you can do it because you aren't just yourself. You're everyone who ever sang "Finnegan's Wake," so of course you can slam through the song on a borrowed guitar and win the mickey of Irish whiskey and get your name in the paper: "Local Teacher Wins St. Patrick's Day Contest."

Yes, the memories come welling up. They have to be brutally suppressed. But before I go on, I have to say I'm really tired of the insignificance of all this. Just once in my life I want to be in on a big one. So **Blow, winds, and crack your cheeks!** That's it. Wouldn't Shakespeare just have loved the bold face.

An absence of patter. I think so, anyway. Absence of patter, but not, I'm sorry to say, absence of speech. What did I say? Whatever, it did me no credit. Not a peep from the audience. When you die, they die. Patter, a little player-people natter, it puts everyone at ease. Some players, you actually like it when they, say, break a string, because hey! they broke strings in every club from here to The Fat Cat and replacing the string with that crank they keep in their case just gives them time to remember Son House, that helluva night in Robinsonville when he broke *two* damn strings on the same damn thrash and never missed a—can you believe it?—never missed a beat, just went to thumpin' out a bass drone while he retuned the other four strings. Unbefuckinglievable. No, your true players don't need patter. I shouldn't have called it patter. Patter—that was Leonard Cohen in concert in the 1970s: the exact same lines on the stage in London and Toronto and what really made you wonder was why one of the backup singers was slapping her knee so hard at the identical jokes both times. Was knee-slapping in the script? Patter. I would've *used* patter. It was me causing the squawk of feedback once I got the chair set up again. It's you, Stan, Gerry said from behind the console. Move back from the mike. And I really wish my capo hadn't fallen apart just then. If the rubber backing on the neck bit hadn't fallen off we could at least have gone smoothly into "Bald Prairie," Jill and I. My singing was over, public singing completely over once and forever. All I had to do was pick out "Bald Prairie" and Jill would sing it and what little attention there was left to pay would be paid to her. But the pesky little rubber piece that had stayed loyal just like my left hand through a billion hours of playing at home in the bedroom with the door shut tight fell off and rolled away. *Real* musicians at that point, they just transpose the key, but there's a minor chord in "Bald Prairie," and something else a ways up the neck that I don't even know the name of. It's not that easy to scoop up a little piece of rubber off the floor while keeping your ass stuck on a gimcrack tripod that has already let you down once tonight. Forget about graceful. Forget about "moving right along." Without Crazy Glue you can count on about fifteen minutes to fiddle the rubber piece back into place between the neck and the clamp and . . . Almost nobody who was there that night is left in town. But I won't feel right about it until all of those same people are dead.

&

There's a poplar tree
Waiting for me
Out where the prairie rolls
(Don't the prairie roll)
    & the beauty of that place
    Is that the whole human race
    Is just me
        & when that evening sun goes down
        I go out & ramble around
        Just me & my tree
        The bald prairie
        In harmony

There's a poplar tree &c
    & There's a coyote howls
    She never scowls
    At me

There's a poplar &c
    & There's a magpie squawks
    I hear him talking
    To me

There's &c
    & There's a gopher squeaks
    I see her peeking
    At me

        O it's so good to be alone

I got everywhere to roam
There's me & my gopher
Me & my magpie
Me & my coyote
Me & my tree
& the bald prairie
In harmoneeee

Kenneth Arthur Dragland
1911–1981

L

the fire that breaks from thee then

In 1978 David Young organized a seminar on the teaching of creative writing to coincide with Coach House's parade of authors, Revenge of the Big Sonnet. The seminar speakers were Robert Kroetsch and Ed Dorn. Dorn, scarcer in this country than Kroetsch, was the luminary of the afternoon and the final reader at the Sonnet itself the following evening. The old Canadian defer-to-the-foreign-star syndrome, I suppose, but it was good to have Dorn among us.

Other members of the seminar were Canadian writers of substance, but, as I look back, Roy Kiyooka is the one who really stands out. He was silent for almost the whole session, then he blew up.

Here was Dorn, not looking quite so much the outlaw as on the back cover of *Slinger*, but tall and craggy and attractive, Dorn explaining his system of grading creative writing: C for good attendance, B for adequate, A for good. Dorn, whose Universe City in *Slinger*, that interstellar philosophical drug-western, is a decreative suburb. Well, it was naive to expect Dorn to be packing. The disquisition on grading wasn't what set Roy off, though it must have contributed: But what about the fucking . . . , he sputtered, I mean, what about the years and years . . . What about the dedication, he was saying, what about pouring your whole life into your work? Don't we teach that? He mentioned his own writing on Tom Thomson. The example holds; twenty-five years later it still isn't published.

Everything about the seminar up to this outburst had been practical, maybe useful, though Dorn's grading system is all that stayed with me. Everything had been comfortable. Suddenly there was heat in the room and the centre of gravity shifted to Roy. Defensive and placating words directed at him were admitting that the passionate heart of the subject had indeed been absent. I see this with hindsight. I didn't agree with Roy then. I thought the lifelong wrestle with words could be assumed. Well, I've changed my mind, but it's not the words I value from that afternoon so much as Roy Kiyooka himself, sprung rhythm.

I knew who Roy Kiyooka was at the time, not much more. I remember picking up *StonedGloves* in bookstores, looking at the pictures and wondering. I never bought one. By the time of the seminar I had a copy of *transcanada letters* but had only flipped through it. I didn't know much.

It took me quite a few years to catch up with Roy's passion, but the bang of his reading at Revenge of the Big Sonnet was immediate:

> aphasia a cross the frozen stubble
> aphasia of his Famine
> aphasia the drifting snow-mantl'd pasture broke n
> aphasia down the huge hole
> aphasia Black. root. **pie** in the sky
>
> aphasia . . .

I don't remember what Dorn read, except that it was funny, intelligent, and brief. Other than the collaborative piece by Christopher Dewdney and Robert Fones designed to insult most of the writers in the audience, what I remember best of the Big Sonnet was Roy Kiyooka compelling attention, burning through those riveting lines of non-sense.

◄○►

Eventually I met Roy, at the house of a mutual friend. Happy to listen, I spoke very little on that occasion. I remember his marvelling that the University of BC actually paid him to talk about the art he was living. I liked the way he laughed, holding his sides and toppling over sideways on the couch. I found little more to say the one time Roy and I had a few minutes by ourselves, at the 1991 bpNichol conference in Vancouver. I hadn't thought shyness was an affliction Roy shared with me, but he was quiet that time too. Conversation didn't flow. He gave me a copy of *The Capilano Review* with the wonderful text/photograph elegy for his mother in it.

Surely we could have gotten going, Roy and I. His was the one letter about my *Journeys Through Bookland* that came right out of the blue. He wrote from the West Coast to me in Ontario about our mutual love of the prairies. To me he was exotic—not because he was Japanese, but because of those wonderfully independent texts, *StonedGloves* and *transcanada letters* and *The Fontainebleu Dream Machine*—and I was touched that he had liked my own straight writing about Alberta. But we never got talking when we had the chance. I didn't know him and yet, one of the pure ones, he was immensely important to me.

◄○►

First and second readings of Daphne Marlatt's *Zócalo*:

1. The narrator is travelling with this, yes, inscrutable oriental man. He doesn't say much; he isn't as dead set on seeing all the Yucatan sights as she is, doesn't bother with the guidebook. He seems the ultimate

antitourist in fact, sufficient in himself, content just to hang out in this foreign country, a sort of lamp of reason that the narrator flutters around. Yo is his name, short for Yoshio, but he's Roy Kiyooka, as the narrator is a mask of Daphne Marlatt in the first phase of the search for her mother. Yo takes photographs all the time. This might be a version of the male gaze; anyway, the eye looks cold.

This guy is a withholder. Identifying with the narrator, his partner—twitching to her nerve-end sensitivities—I'm not sure I like him. He won't help her worry and she worries about everything.

2. Just a minute. There is no other point of view than the narrator's here. The withholder has to be her, or else the author. If you don't write from inside him, of course he will look flat. But *Zócalo* is not about him; it's about her. There is somewhere inside herself she has to go. She has to revisit the scene of some dreadful damage, and her sentences are minutely, precisely, looping their way towards it. It's not about him, but when the time comes for her falling inward, he turns out not to be the lamp of reason she thought he was, that she was in fact counting on him to be. Her selective reading of him is one of those fictions we invent to keep our partners slotted, neatly othered against us. He reads her nightmare perfectly, intuitively, and thus allows her to fall away from him towards where she has to go.

◄o►

It must happen everywhere (it happens plenty in Canada) that writers write their partners into print and then suffer a split so that nobody can revisit those texts of love without pain. It's an occupational hazard of publishing what you care most about that your pain as sure as your love hangs out for everyone to see. Writers manage separation no better than others, except that it helps to have an instrument tuned and ready. Roy Kiyooka's *Pear Tree Pomes* is addressed to Daphne Marlatt:

> since you and i forsook the rites of marriage
>
> intentionally without - facing up to the signals of mutual
> disenchantment - we found ourselves side-stepping
> each other's nakedness to fall asleep in a heap of mired feelings
> til the early bird traffic on prior street summoned us
> to another "good morning - did you sleep well" breakfast
> on the run . there's a lady with a champagne voice on co-op radio
> singin' the ol' after midnight blues and whoops! - there's
> that ol' heart-ache again . what I want to know is how come you
> with your bright gists and me with my pointed beard didn't
> make the perfect match . how come we ended up playing
> that ol' deaf and dumb game when it was as plain as this prose
> that the pear tree's forkt branches foretold the truth .
> since you left i've been taking a hot water bottle to bed
>   how about you with your tepid toes?

Pear Tree Pomes grows sweetly out of pain into offering, for the reader as well as the dear, departed.

—◄o►—

A postcard has slipped behind the chalkboard above the phone in my kitchen. I won't forget it's there. I won't ever forget what's on it: a word spoken of me by Roy Kiyooka and passed along by the friend in whose house we met.

&

A Big One

M

Mountain Railroad

> This may be gossip,
> but that doesn't make it unimportant.
>
> Bronwen Wallace, "Place of Origin"

Bronwen and I never really got to know each other, but we do have a longish history. It goes back to graduate school—Queen's University in 1969. In my mind it goes back to a seminar room on the fifth floor of Watson Hall, Bron and I both members of a class listening to the professor talk. He is a full professor, which means that whenever a new idea goes in an old one slides out. This particular professor is interesting, though, and easy to follow, so easy in fact that Bron sees where he's going, puts up her hand, and makes his next big point for him.

I know, he snaps.

It was a vividly educational moment.

Bron dropped out of the PhD program, and I saw very little of her until, nineteen years later, she became writer-in-residence at Western, my university. Then she told me, more than once, the story of dropping out, raging out, leaving behind an indictment of the system addressed to another professor, one I admired hugely. What was in that letter? I have to guess. I'd say the total inadequacy of criticism for dealing with literature, the unconscionable gap between literary criticism and real life.

—◄○►—

A couple of doors down from the office of the chair of Western's Graduate Studies in English, directly across from the office of Department Chair, is the office where Bron met student writers in 1988. The pastel-on-black velvet portrait of Elvis that she put up just inside the door hung there after she was gone. She left it for her successor, Tim Lilburn, to salute his "Elvis" poem, "Travelling Among the Energies of the Dead." The King is depicted in his later years—after he started performing in the rhinestone jumpsuit, but before he was a size forty-eight. Elvis got me started too, so I got ready to remove that portrait before the wall it was on got knocked out. It hung through Tim Lilburn, Margaret Hollingsworth, and Leon Rooke, and I let it hang through Christopher Dewdney, because I stayed in the PhD program at Queen's, and I'm trained to recognize shades and layers of irony.

—◄○►—

After dinner at our place, we lingered over the rest of the wine, and Bron told once again the story of dropping out of Queen's. I listened silently, wondering why this was coming up again. I was too defensive to respond as I should have, whether or not Bron was inviting it. You were right, Bron, I should have said, you did the right thing. It didn't have to mean I'd done the wrong thing, after all. I should have said that I liked her writing, and that I was in awe of the way she connected with people—joking, gossiping, monitoring Elvis sightings, listening with her whole self—it takes one of her own long looping sentences to fit it all in, all of it sounding like casual conversation, but it was really healing. She was finding the best in people as well as in their writing, giving them nonauthoritative permission to be what they really wanted to be, which was often enough not an academic; she was creating a community out of talk. I was jealous of how useful she'd made her life.

While Bron did the dishes, Marnie and I sang for her. There was no tension between us on the subject of Emmylou Harris and country gospel. I may have missed every chance to say the things I should have said, but I was able to sing.

> Life is like a mountain railroad
> With an engineer so brave.
> We must make this run successful
> From the cradle to the grave.
> Watch the curves, beware the tunnel.
> Never falter, never fail,
> With your hand upon the throttle
> And your eye upon the rail.

Perhaps Bron could hear that verse the way it should be sung, the way I always hear it, with the lead singer just a-honkin and the group humming, moaning in harmony back there, getting ready to open their throats for the Jesus chorus. I learned the song from a man who thought it was a joke, but I've been singing it with joy, without irony, for many years. Drawn in unfaith to words and melody that plain faith created. Saying too late, Bron, I believe in you.

&

I believe in Bronwen's feminist activism, yes. I believe in her poems as well, though I didn't like the way she read them. I thought her quiet words would stand without the artificial boost she gave them, reading in such a breathless rush.

But we didn't get to know one another because we took a scunner to each other. There are times to suppress antipathy in the interests of a common cause or out of respect not born of love, but it's not good to conceal real & reasonable reasons for it from yourself. I thought Bronwen got lost in the temporary rebellions of the 1960s, when students grabbed & held enormous power over their teachers. Queen's University had its very own show trial—a graduate student of engineering accused his supervisor of unfair treatment and the student activists turned the resulting enquiry into a trial of Western society—& Bronwen's role was to show up in whiteface with a group of like minds to disrupt the inquiry itself, a tool of The Man. Myself, I sat night after night at the enquiry, torn & wondering, drawn neither to the defensive university establishment nor the wide-eyed student radicals.

Bronwen knew what side she was on. I instinctively mistrusted her single-mindedness. It didn't last. Poetry returned her to complexity. She didn't become what Guy Davenport says e.e. cummings did, "the usual crank the young red-bonneted rebel ages into." But she was no kindred spirit, even when I sang for her, not even by her deathbed, where I felt hypocritical. I hadn't earned the visit I made with Marnie. A part of me I didn't like was still holding out.

N

Les Arnold in London (Ont.)

"The local is the only universal." Les had that from William Carlos Williams. I think Les believed that a poet had to stand in a place he understood, in its layers of history, geography, cosmos. He had to *be* one of those layers. There was Paterson, New Jersey (Williams); there was Gloucester, Massachusetts (Olson). Not just places, but poems with a human backbone. There was London, Ontario. A second London, with another Thames River flowing through it. That's where Les lived when I met him, first on Colborne St., named after a colonel, a colonizer whose feet had at least touched local ground. Gloucester is an English name too, but somehow the old overlay on the new place is less thick, less heavy when shrugged off by revolution, when its poet-resident reaches out for the universe. Some poets, rooted, bring everything home.

Les wanted to be at home in London, and that wasn't easy. He and Sandy moved to an acreage outside the city on the Waubomin Creek, tributary to the Thames, which we find, digging down, the Neutral Indians called Askunessippi, Antler River. (Doing his own digging, Greg Curnoe discovered that London was first called Pahkatequayaug, "where there is a lot of people.") Les began to look into the area's history. He built a barn and raised sheep. He was teaching English at the University of Western Ontario as well, but he saw himself as peripheral to academe, at least to "the English Department of the Spirit," in Jack Spicer's acid phrase, "that great quagmire that lurks at the bottom of all of us." When Les quit, he was quoted in the student newspaper to the effect that only three or four people in the English Department were actually alive. The remark was not resented; every department member counted him or herself among the living few.

I knew something of what Les was going through in trying to adapt to London. My own upbringing was Albertan. A prairie boy doesn't fit smoothly and inevitably into Ontario, the history and the landscape being vastly different. I found London difficult to connect with, though I also found that Ontario difference unlocked my prairie self and I began to write about that. If dislocations worked the same way for everyone, Les would have been writing about England—about Blackpool, perhaps. But he was an Englishman pulled to the New World. He was drawn to American poetry. He taught it and wrote about it. I think he wanted to write it. London is not Paterson; Canada is not the United States. There were indigenous complexities difficult to surmount. I still have a T-shirt Les gave me. He had "The Waubomin Flows Here" inscribed across the chest. A man, wearing it, should have been a creek. I think he gave the shirt away knowing he'd been trying too hard.

Perhaps the return to England was inevitable. Les *was* English. He played some soccer for London's German Canadian Club, but he felt more at home with St. George's. When he'd been back in England for a few years, he sent me a collection of Moschatel Press mini-books and printed cards by Laurie and Thomas A. Clark, little treasures that are as eloquently and sophisticatedly rural as anything I've ever seen. "Childbirth," the poem dedicated to the Clarks, and "Apology for Country Poems," both in *Joy Riding*, show me that Les ended where he belonged as a poet. I may be making too much of a detail in Les's English life, which I never saw at first hand, but if I find those Moschatel productions sustaining over here, how much more so must they have been to Les, they and the rich rural English grain.

─◄o►─

Les was restless, always full of energy. Driven. Ambitious? If so, only as a poet. He was obsessive about poetry. I sometimes felt that his writing reflected that obsession to its detriment. Poems about writing poems are still there in his last book, *Joy Riding* (in which space was found for the last poem he wrote, about proofreading the volume), but now they are naturalized in the wordscape. This is an earned and integral reflexivity.

What was driving him? I don't know. His friendship was generous, but it had an opacity to it. He did surprise me by confiding not long before he and Sandy returned to England that he wasn't intellectually confident. I can't remember, but I hope I said Welcome to the club. There was nothing wrong with his mind, though he wasn't cut out to be a mainstream academic. He was a dynamic teacher, a terrific actor, an excellent director (if rather cavalier with the acquisition of rights: deep into rehearsal, his English Department production of *The Real Inspector Hound* was shut down for lack of them).

It sometimes seemed to me that Les was avid for more experience than he then had the inner workings to absorb. I remember him trying out his new fly-fishing kit in the creek by our cottage. I doubt that Depot Creek had the kind of fish that would rise to a fly, but never mind; not every fisher actually cares for the catching. Les was having trouble gentling that line out. He was using his rod like a whip. He'd have gotten it eventually, but in the meantime you could see his impatience churning. It wasn't unusual to see that.

◄o►

Because he was always such a dervish of energy, his death is hard to handle. The last time I saw him in London, visiting his father who'd settled here, he hadn't changed an iota. After ten years, you expect some alteration, but he hadn't put a pound on that athletic body and his hair was still crow-black. He was clearly not burning himself out. Reading "Health," the last section of *Joy Riding*, I remembered some lines from "In Laughter," a poem in Ted Hughes's *Crow* that's anything but funny: "In laughter, in laughter/ The meteorite crashes/ With extraordinarily ill luck on the pram." Would Les have felt, as it's often tough not to feel, that absurd early deaths such as his could happen only in a senseless existence? Maybe not. *Joy Riding* speaks out of a sense of settlement which makes it natural to rage at human idiocy, but in which death is natural too.

Joy Riding is a satisfying summation of what ought to have been a stage of his poetic life. It has to be the whole poetic legacy now, but as such it will stand.

◄o►

Sometime in 1971, Les pounced on the envelope I was leaving in the English Department mail drop. He could spot a brown 8 1/2 x 11 envelope addressed to a little magazine across a crowded room. Les hauled me out of the closet that day, and so began our association in poetry. Les was sending out his poems too. He showed me with glee the tersest rejection slip I've ever seen: "Sorry."

How it was that a few of us (Don McKay, Allan Gedalof, Les,

and myself) got together to set up as publishers is a wrinkled tale unnecessary to tell. So is a tangent, my own life in publishing begun with that misguided effort. Clean. Snatch. Jerk n' Press, we called it. We handset Les's *Black Jack Crow: Song and Dance Man* (1973) and printed it, perhaps 100 copies, on the English Department's old jobber. Collectors may know of this book as (content aside) probably the ugliest slim volume ever produced. What were we thinking when we chose that dreadful maroon cover paper? Why would we repeat the aesthetic outrage in the middle of the book (four central maroon pages turning into five because no one thought to make a dummy and we ended up a page short which we had to tip in)? I felt and still feel much better about Les's *Notes on the Paintings of Francis Bacon*, a decently designed chapbook that I published under the Nairn imprint in 1978. That sequence joined others in a manuscript called *winterpoems*, an early gathering like *Joy Riding* that was not, as far as I know, published. The section of *winterpoems* entitled "The Relatives" bears this as epigraph:

> The relatives said
> You'll go far Les & I
> did I came to Canada
> But I'm going back
> to Visit (once I
> remember which country
> I left them in:

—◁o▷—

Les and I not only hung out as writers. With Penny and Sandy, we were friends. Friends are the ones you ask to help you paper the ceiling of the upstairs bedroom in the Colborne St. house. Is it wise to paper ceilings? I think not. If it were, "ceilingpaper" would be a word. How do you hold the damn strips of paper up? Les and I stood, one on a table and one on a chair, with a strip of wallpaper sagging between us. Sandy brought a sponge mop to support the middle, but she pressed too hard and the mop slipped away and struck Les a terrible blow on the forehead. It should have knocked him out. Maybe it was the incongruity between that thwack and Les's mere (but intense) annoyance—he never even dropped his end—that made Sandy and I begin to giggle and to keep on giggling well past the point when it became clear that Les was not going to join in.

Les wasn't being hard-headed the night he raced over to catch Penny and me before we left for the hospital where she gave birth to our first child. He brought us a little sealskin doll. Perched on the edge of the bed in the upstairs bedroom of the townhouse in Berkshire Village, he was shining. He wasn't much less excited than we were. What had we done to inspire such love?

Les was *more* than we were—more intense, more generous, more subversive, more theatrical. No wonder he's still alive in me.

&

Foliations

Lintel Laurel
Mullion Mullein
Quatrefoil Cinquefoil
Campanile Campanula

        Thomas A. Clark

O

Walt Whitman's Niece

On Sunday, March 14, 1999, I saw a man go into the Jumbo Video at Wharncliffe and Baseline. He was wearing a sweater with horizontal bands of orange, yellow, red, and blue. No, this was not a spectral vision of Greg Curnoe, but I did think at the time that no one but Greg could look natural in such a getup. I believe Greg's guts were those colours. I know his opinions were: loud and plain and bright. He used to come to Forest City Gallery meetings wearing those guts and opinions, with red suspenders, and make motions out of whatever popped into his mind. Some of us had heard rumours of *Robert's Rules of Order*. What we had, most meetings, was Curnoe's Nihilist Spasm. Goddamn it to hell, I thought on many evenings, here we go again, here we go 'round the fucking mulberry bush. I liked those mental spasms way better at Greg and Sheila's place. In conversation they always created an edge that could hone my own drab ideas. Talking to Greg always woke me up.

In the early 1970s Greg was giving a reading from the journal he kept on a Spasm Band tour in Britain. After the applause, Sheila stood up to find that her coat had slipped off the back of her chair. One of the chair legs was standing on it. She was pissed off at the indignity to her good leather coat and she swore at the chair. We hadn't met then, but she smiled at me as she cursed. That moment survives in my memory when millions of others are lost because

Sheila fills a moment with her personality. I never thought of her as standing in Greg's shadow—she's too bright—though he always drew a lot of attention. Someday, I'll try to recount the true story Sheila once told of a young woman killed by lightning at a horse show on the edge of London. The lightning seared off her clothes but didn't mark her body. She was beautiful, dead, and nude. It wouldn't be easy to tell that story properly, though I have Sheila's permission, because I can't detach it from Sheila—her wonder at the arbitrary selectiveness of that power. All of us around the table with our wine glasses full, drawn together by the story. Wondering, with Sheila—*why?*

Katherine Mansfield's "The Wind Blows" has one of the best short-story endings ever. One minute the adolescent narrator and her brother are watching this big black steamer cutting through the wind as it leaves the harbour, leaving New Zealand; next moment they are *on* that steamer, years later, and waving. "Good-bye, little island, good-bye." I went straight from Marion Johnston's invitation to say something about Greg Curnoe and I wrote that down. So who am I to say, months later, that it has nothing to do with Greg? Well, sez you, somebody should! So I'd better push the thought: Greg was, and is, at the beating heart of the city I'm leaving after twenty-nine years. Greg Curnoe, Ron and Tom Benner, Jack Chambers, Murray Favro, Jamelie Hassan, James Reaney, Colleen Thibaudeau. I could go on. Heart of London. Goodbye, Souwesto, goodbye.

March 14, 1999. Marnie puts on Billy Bragg and Wilco singing Bragg's music for Woody Guthrie's lyric, "Walt Whitman's Niece." The song takes the old form of call and response. Billy Bragg sings a line ("Last night or the night before that") and the chorus responds in harmony ("I won't say which night"). I don't understand why such joy stabs me, listening to this song, but new life for Woody Guthrie must be part of it. Woody Guthrie and Walt Whitman. A live community joyfully haunted by the so-called dead. "For Black Blooms," says Christopher Smart, "and it is PURPLE." Along with everything bright, Sheila, here in the Forest City community Greg helped to found, I'm holding on to something royal, pulsing, a band of purple, indigo. We all are.

on the afternoon of November 13, 1992, while we watched the Santa Claus parade moving through downtown London, Greg Curnoe was riding with the Centennial Wheelers on a regular weekend chase over county roads north of town. He'd been leading the pack &, in the usual drill, had just dropped to the rear when a truck ploughed into the line of cyclists from behind. There were several injuries, but Greg was the only rider killed. Aged fifty-six, at the top of his form.

P

Typing, Writing, "Racial Memories"

> I patched my coat with darkness:
> That coat has kept me warm.
>
> Dennis Lee, "The Coat"

Asked to write something about Matt Cohen, I knew right away that I wanted to do two things. One was to write something about the Matt I was friendly with for about twenty-five years. The other was to explore his short story, "Racial Memories." I didn't at first see how these two aims could be connected. I found that I couldn't write anything like an essay about our association because we hung out only sporadically. I saw Matt and Patsy and the kids mainly in the summers over about twenty-five years, from sometime before 1980 until his death in 2000, when we lived near each other north of Kingston, Ontario. Some tennis-playing summers Matt and I saw quite a lot of each other. Later, it might be a family cottage-to-cabin meal exchange; later still, just Matt for a meal at our place once a summer, not even that when they were in France. Matt and I were friends, I think, but never intimate. So I have glimpses rather than a continuum. My two subjects do now meet in Matt's posthumous memoir, *Typing: A Life in 26 Keys*, which I read with the intention of checking my own fallible memory. It turns out that *Typing* barely touches the eastern Ontario Matt and I shared, but it does show me a Matt Cohen very different from the one I thought I knew, one who is palpably the author of "Racial Memories," the Cohen story I most admire. When I told Matt how much I liked it, he went still. He seemed to retreat into himself for a moment. I've wondered since if it was because I hadn't praised his writing before.

I might have known Matt better if I'd been keeping up with his work. "I'm convinced that there are intimate ties between what people propose to themselves as their so-called rational thoughts and what they imagine," he says in *Typing*. But I wasn't taken with the Salem novels and never got back into reading Cohen until it was too late to connect with the man through the books.

And now I have these misgivings, wondering if the Matt Cohen I remember is the real one. It's a tortured, cynical, even nihilistic Matt Cohen who appears in *Typing*. There was a foreignness, a mis-fit to him that I never picked up on. Not the sort of thing you find out playing tennis and socializing. And the fiction doesn't contradict that, not even the comic stories. Well, *Typing* is not the whole picture. It's prefaced with a note by Patsy Aldana: "Anyone who knew Matt will notice that many important people and events in his life cannot be found in this book. They will also know how rich and complex his nonwriting life was." So there's a selectiveness unsurprising in writing produced under sentence of death. And there's invention as well: "When I started writing this memoir," Matt says at the beginning of the last chapter, "I was curious to know what narrator would invent himself, what story he would tell and through what kind of lens he would view the past." This doesn't mean that *Typing* was made up; it's a reminder of the need to choose between many possible angles to tell any story, fictional or nonfictional. The Matt who wrote *Typing* would be unlikely to write a jolly, upbeat memoir under any conditions, but he wasn't always living near the abyss, not in my experience.

I

> The small community of Bellrock is close to Verona which is northwest of Kingston. The painter Kim Ondaatje has a summer home at Bellrock and here Michael Ondaatje (b. 1943) and D.G. Jones (b. 1928) have written some of their finest poems. Other residents of the region are two academic critics, Stan Dragland (b. 1942), author of the autobiographical novel *Peckertracks: a Chronicle* (1978), and John Moss (b. 1940), author of *A Reader's Guide to the Canadian Novel* (1983). The novelist Matt Cohen (b. 1942) lives in nearby Verona, features of which appear in his fiction as "Salem."
> (John Robert Colombo)

This is obsolete and was inaccurate even when it appeared. All of those mentioned once had Bellrock in common, but John and Ginny Moss were the only ones to live in the village—at the edge of it, actually, on Goose Island in Depot Creek. Matt picked up his mail in Verona, but he was living on the Chameau Road north of Bellrock, while the others mentioned merely summered along the parallel First Lake Road. Except for D.G. Jones. He and Monique Grandmangin would drive over from North Hatley, Quebec, once a summer. In an Author's Note to *Flowers of Darkness*, Matt bids goodbye to "the fictional town of Salem" from another fictional town, Chameauxville, that he invented for fun out of Chameau Road, no doubt with visions of camels dancing in his head.

But Matt's first residence in eastern Ontario, from 1970, was on a farm near Godfrey, which is a few kilometres north of Verona on

Highway 38. So the brief biographies say, anyway. Godfrey may have been the nearest postal address, because I've long had the impression that the farm was east of Godfrey along the Westport Road. This is the place he speaks of in *Typing*: "I loved it more than any place I had ever lived, and felt truly at home for the first time in my life." Westport was the nearest good-sized community and I've understood it to be more of a model for the fictional Salem than any other particular place. The actual town is only a source to be transformed at need, and it has much in common with other small communities in the area—Verona, Harrowsmith, Sydenham, even tiny Bellrock—but there it is again in *Elizabeth and After*, Westport now recognizable in West Gull, "a small farming centre and tourist town that for almost two centuries had been clinging to the shore of Long Gull Lake, an elongated granite-shored dip on the southern edge of the Precambrian Shield." There is an actual Salem—little more than a name now—still on the map just west of Westport. I haul the garbage from our present cottage on Thirteen Island Lake to the Salem dump. A twinkle appeared in Matt's eye when I told him that. I'd known him for years before he had any occasion to mention where he got the name. Of course, where is less significant than why: the gothic intensity associated with the Massachussetts town of the same name.

Matt moved to the Chameau Road cabin in 1978, spent the winter there without power, and eventually added on to it in stages. It's the model for the cabin in *Last Seen*, "a ramshackle half-built warning to would-be city handymen that Alec bought and began piecing together just before he met Margaret." Matt's own cabin was pretty well pieced together, and the first stage of expansion completed, before I met him. The clincher is "the fact that [Alec's] lawnmowers aren't used on lawn—there is none—but on whatever grass, sumac roots, small cherry or poplar saplings as well as other unidentified sticks, flowers or rocky outcroppings he can get at before he either shears off the blade, runs out of gas or is driven inside by blackflies." It's interesting to see the place through the lens of Matt's irony. He didn't feel ironic about it. Lawn is for cities, suburbs. If even a property, moved into fiction, takes on a tone foreign to the proprietor, a reader had better check any impulse to gauge the character of the author by what he writes.

Matt's cabin is beautifully situated—very private, well off the Chameau Road and surrounded by trees. The property adjoins a tract of Crown land that Matt liked to ramble over. One of the first things we did together was walk from his place through the woods past the beaver pond to the spot near Depot Creek where I'd set up a dining tent to write in. We found a log spanning the creek below the cottage I was renting then. I have a photograph of Matt on that log. I thought there was a good chance he'd slip off it and I got ready to record the moment. That was before the years when he was beating the hell out of me at tennis. I might never have figured him for an athlete if I hadn't seen him in action because he generally moved a bit stiffly, as though not fully at ease in his body.

Matt had been living in his cabin for some years before I met him, year-round for much of that time. I know he cared for the place and its surroundings, so I know that he left much of real importance out of *Typing*. I'd say he puts the stress on Ottawa, then Toronto, and the Westport area farm because they were formative and he was undergoing sometimes extreme turmoil in them. He was solitary when I met him, but apparently stable, and it wasn't too much longer before he found an anchor in Patsy Aldana and became a stepfather and a father and lived, externally at least, a relatively settled life that increasingly alternated between the cabin and Toronto, eventually between Canada and France. He'd often be alone in the cabin for long stretches of the summer (fine for a writer) because Patsy's publishing work was in the city and she never became the country person Matt did.

"Acting on people the land created a body of lore," says John Steffler's George Cartwright in the novel bearing his name, "a system of plots like a second geography. And like rivers and coasts the lore continued to shape people's fates." The artists of "Frontenac County, a narrow, jagged rectangle of rocky shield, swamps and lakes that begins at Kingston and stretches north well past Highway 7," have marked the place as it marked them, whether lightly or indelibly. Subtract D.G. Jones from Colombo's piece and add Kit Chubb, Joan Finnigan, Kim Ondaatje, Dorothy Murray Sliter, Carolyn Smart, and Bronwen Wallace. It hasn't been for long that one could say of an Ontario subregion like the country north of Kingston that its history and geography has attracted a palimpsest, a pentimento of fiction, poetry, nonfiction, and film. I'm an Alberta writer who lived for almost thirty years in London, Ontario, whose Ontario roots are in South Frontenac Township, who has now come under the powerful influence of Newfoundland. Matt Cohen was an eastern Ontario writer profoundly influenced by Europe, by France and Spain from medieval to modern times. Few of the writers named are limited to Frontenac County either in experience or writing, but the area is important to them.

A stickler, a map-lover like Vladimir Nabokov, might wish to nuance Matt's geography. Topographical maps show that the marginal country he speaks of begins in earnest not immediately north of Kingston, but north of a ragged forty-kilometre line west to east through places like Enterprise, Moscow, Petworth, Hartington, Sydenham, Inverary, and Battersea. The Geological Highway Map of Southern Ontario shows Shield emerging from more southerly limestone along this line. Once this was lumbering country, mining country. See Michael Ondaatje's poems "Walking to Bellrock" and "Pig Glass" and the Bellrock sections of *In the Skin of a Lion*. It was always marginal for agriculture, failure in which produced "the abandoned foundations of the houses and barns built by the families who had tried to settle there, all of whose histories and tragedies [Matt] knew, thanks to the neighbours" (*Typing*). For the critic as for the writer, geography is not mere ground, not setting only. This is not the place to read Matt's novels for their record of characters *made* marginal by the land they lived on, nor to read the region in the light of Matt's novels, but a long-standing seasonal resident of that region may be justified in calling for such reciprocation.

In number 14 of *Brick* magazine (1982), Jean McKay and I published Ann Gunnarson's review of Don Coles's *Sometimes All Over*. Ann Gunnarson is the pseudonym of a writer who wanted to salute a remarkable book without calling attention to himself. This was perfectly understandable in a man known to be one of the best editors in Canada, a man far too generous with his time for his own good. Jean and I were happy to oblige. We too found it inconvenient to be nobody but ourselves. But maybe the reviewer should have altered his distinctive style as well as his name. The attentive reader's ears might well have perked up the minute s/he saw the experience of falling in love called "a doozer." Anyway, Matt wasn't fooled. In fact he thought the spectacle of Dennis Lee hiding right out in the open was hilarious. Invited, as one of the earliest Anansi writers, to write about Lee's editing for *Tasks of Passion: Dennis Lee at Mid-Career*, Matt began by recounting a telephone conversation about Dennis

Lee with Ann Gunnarson. So a serious act of concealment turned into an in-joke.

Matt had his own ways of hiding, as in the evasive introduction to *Café Le Dog*. The author's muse is presented as a character out of a novel too good to publish. Now she's out to seduce him—which is right. But she's not believable as muse; she's a device to get some editor off the author's back: "The editor told me I should write about the difference between novels and short stories." His muse says she "had exactly the same topic in Grade Twelve English." So much for the editor, who probably hoped for more than a Grade Twelve essay from the author (by 1985) of several novels and two other collections of short stories. All he gets is what the muse dictates: "You see, honey, a novel is like one of those boring old-fashioned marriages, but a short story is a one night stand." A sleazy muse. This goes nowhere. Nowhere is a common place and a good place to start. It's exactly where you're left by one of those rare serious, beautiful, probing, truly seductive author statements—*in* that writing, ready to follow the writer anywhere.

Matt used the evasive strategy of irony in conversation. Maybe it was habitual. In *Typing* he refers to the "political meetings of the [1960s] left" as "the perfect format for shallow anarchistic types (such as myself) for whom the height of political wisdom was to throw digressive one-liners into the discussion that made everyone forget whatever it was they were attempting to discuss." There's a parallel "digression technique" in *Last Seen*, which might be titled "How to Destroy a Story Told by Someone You Can't Stand." My own pleasure in non sequitur is hospitable to digressive riffing. A whole goddamn conversation might so honour the red herring as to leave you feeling hollow. I'd better be careful saying that I sometimes found Matt's evasions annoying since I have my own instinctive tricks. I suppose there's a bittersweet masculine comedy here: two guys hanging out for years, both of them with lots going on inside their heads and keeping most of it right in there.

Since we weren't intimate, I don't know how much of Matt's evasion was natural, how much cultivated. Maybe he cherished his reserve as little as I do mine, but I find reserve in most of his stories: archness, pose, narrators slightly distanced, world-weary, and ironic. No wonder Anna Porter said to him: "Why don't you write something that reveals more about yourself. Your books are always so distant. Why don't you write something about being Jewish" (*Typing*). Ironically, Matt was already in a position to offer her the idea for *The Spanish Doctor,* which is about being Jewish but hardly a self-portrait. *Nadine* and *Emotional Arithmetic* were to follow, but Anna Porter's challenge gets perhaps its straightest response in "Racial Memories."

2

Here are the important things I didn't know about Matt; I give them more emphasis than might someone who wasn't a friend, but I don't see how they could be missed by anyone reading the whole of *Typing*. One thing is the strained relationship with his father, a scientific rationalist whose stance Matt expresses thus: "Everyone knew the study of arts was reserved for those whose brains and psyches were too feeble to tear off the blinders of superstition and ignorance, get out their slide rules and figure out how the universe worked." "I was going to study science," Matt says of his initial intentions at the University of Toronto, "because it might get me my father's approval—I desperately craved it and nothing else had ever worked." Neither did this. Matt transferred out of science and eventually adopted a career his father thought was childish.

Another thing is Matt's eccentric relationship with Judaism. It was not at the core of his parents' life and thus not central to his own. He has nothing to say about being nurtured by Jewish tradition, but he does speak of childhood persecution. Is this why he calls himself a "self-hating Jew"? What he doesn't spell out in *Typing* is clarified by "Racial Memories," but parallel self-hatred is easy to find in other cultures suppressed by a Canadian mainstream or establishment perpetuated by lack of self-examination. Yes, human nature being what it is, there's a bandwagon of whining, self-declared victims, but the real victims aren't on it. Readers of *Obasan* will not be surprised to hear me name Joy Kogawa as an example. Some may consider the racist outrage that *Obasan* documents something of the past, laid to rest by a successful redress movement. But Kogawa is not speaking of internment when, in an *Other Solitudes* interview with Magdalen Redekop, she says, "Almost all of my life I would have done anything to be white, I just wanted it so desperately." There it is: tragic loathing of a self that can't be changed, hatred of what should be neutral if not a source of pride because it doesn't meet the norm, the norm so unquestioned that few notice the damage it does. Until the voices of the "different" begin to be heard.

I'd heard that Matt became a teenage tennis whiz almost in revenge—junior Ontario champion or something like that—because Jews weren't welcome in the country clubs of Ottawa, but he never mentioned anti-Semitism to me. I suppose it was during the post-Salem period that he came to feel his difference as another source of literary exclusion: "Finally I came to understand that *The Spanish Doctor* had come as such a shock to so many of my readers, especially the critics, because of their sense that I had betrayed my Canadianness by writing about being Jewish. It tells you something uncomfortable about people's conception of what it means to be a

Canadian." This is from an interview with Mervyn Butovsky in *Other Solitudes*, an anthology of fiction whose "initial purpose" "was to break through what one commentator [Raymond August] has called 'the protective shell of Canadian-style tolerance: acceptance without concern.'" I discovered "Racial Memories" in this anthology. It was the first Matt Cohen story that grabbed and held, *harrowed* me all the way through, and continues to haunt me.

"Racial Memories" is mentioned early in *Typing*, just once. A long passage describing the grandfather in the story is quoted verbatim as a description of Matt's own paternal grandfather. The context in which the story was written (it was first published in *Living on Water*, 1988) would be interesting to know. But this much is clear: differences and similarities between the narrator of "Racial Memories" and the narrator of *Typing* show that the story is both autobiographical and invented. It stands free as an invention despite the fact that it probes deeply into the author's own psyche—deeper, into communal memory.

I keep coming back to "Racial Memories" with an undiminished sense that it's not only stylistically distinctive and compelling as a narrative, but important, socially useful. Here is Leonard, after all, sometimes repulsive and always monomaniacally Jewish—no kindred spirit of the narrator and not a man I'd care to hang out with. He teaches History at the Orthodox Synagogue Hebrew Day School and his particular obsession is the Holocaust. "Do you think the Holocaust gave the Jews some sort of moral credit card?" asks the narrator in a vain attempt to complicate Leonard's thinking and resist the protest that makes him a martyr to his faith and his race. His death seals a hard lesson. The narrator was right, despite his doubts, to join that protest. Leonard didn't have the whole truth, but he saw that it was crucial to preserve a nasty, unpalatable piece of it.

I don't like Leonard, but I'm with him too, respecting his effort to preserve Jewishness in the face of systemic racist pressure to hide it, to deny, to escape, respecting the conviction that makes him act on what he believes.

There is a legendary escapee in the family. Joseph Lucky, the narrator's ambiguous great-great-uncle and namesake, has somehow made the passage from "the cavalry of the Russian czar" to a ranch in Alberta, "out on the range, riding wild mustangs."

> Somehow he had escaped being Jewish, wiggled out from under his fate and galloped off into that carefree other world where you were not under a life sentence or, to be more exact, perhaps you were under a life sentence of mortality (even an assimilated Jew finds it hard to believe in Heaven) but you had been promoted to a different part of the sentence: instead of being the object, you were the subject.

It's very little to ask, going about as a plain human being, loved or tolerated or hated or ignored as an individual, and not despised for something you can't help, like black skin or eyes with epicanthic folds or same-sex attraction. Some Jews in the story think they *can* help it. The narrator's parents hide out from their Jewishness in Ottawa, at some distance from the immediate family. Eventually his father "decided... to complete his escape and was residing... in Sydney, Australia." Robert Freud, in *Freud: The Paris Notebooks*, goes one better. He "had rejected both religion and reason. He was neither a Jew nor a scientist. He was, he realized with a sudden flush of triumph, nothing at all, just a perpetual foreigner wearing a three-piece suit and inhabiting an office above a bank." Triumph indeed.

In mythic terms, escape to the promised land is supposed to be an option for the Jews. The new world has sometimes looked like a reasonable substitute, but not to the narrator's father, not until he can leave the family far behind. Nor to the son. When childhood friends turn on him and call him "Christ-killer," the heritage of persecution suddenly catches up with him and his life divides. During the day he has to pretend that nothing is amiss, but not at night:

> Then finally the world of fear I'd been containing all day in my belly could expand, spread out, swallow the make-believe theatre of pretend-niceness that surrounded me during the day. In the dark, instead of daring God to show himself as I used to, I listened for the sound of convoy trucks on the road, knocks at the door, policemen's boots on the stairs. And if they weren't going to come? I eventually had to ask myself. Did that mean that in this new world there was safety after all? That my great-great Uncle Joseph Lucky truly had led us out of the wilderness and into the promised land?

If they don't actually show up to take you away, the kid thinks, he might be safe. But "there's no new land, my friend," according to C.P. Cavafy in a poem quoted as epigraph to M.G. Vassanji's, *No New Land*. (Actually, Vassanji's novel matches Cavafy's truth with another, that Canada *is* a new land and a new society that transforms immigrant lives; it's human nature that doesn't change.) The old world of Jew-baiting shows up again and then again in the narrator's adult life. Some promised land that imports such irrational and irrefutable hatred. It would be as presumptuous to criticize anyone for fleeing it as to call Leonard tiresome for keeping the memory of the Holocaust fresh.

The narrator of "Racial Memories" is weighed down by the persecution that erupts in his personal life, but it's not all that parts him from his own tradition. For one thing, he was not raised squarely in it. For another, he has found in his own experience a model of assimilation that is not merely homogenizing, not a denial of all that his people have been and that he therefore still is, but rather an embrace of common humanity. Life founded on the Golden Rule. The promised land in little. His constant best friend since school days has been Peter Riley, the sandy-haired Catholic boy who marries his cousin Laura for love and becomes his law firm partner. Right before his eyes, in those he loves, the narrator sees a viable ecumenical future he cannot enter, not with that heritage of persecution perpetually overtaking him. "'I'm having an identity crisis,' I imagine saying [to a liquor store cashier], 'I mean I was born Jewish but I don't feel comfortable carrying NAZI JEW KILLER signs.'" "I did not like to see the young men stunted in the Polish ghetto," says Leonard Cohen in "Lines From My Grandfather's Journal." "Their curved backs were not beautiful. Forgive me, it gives me no pleasure to see them in uniform. I do not thrill to the sight of Jewish battalions." But the narrator does help carry NAZI JEW KILLER signs to Toronto Airport for the demonstration against the arrival of "an East German cabinet minister someone claims was once a concentration camp guard" because, as Leonard Cohen says in the same poem, "Who dares disdain an answer to the ovens? Any answer." So the narrator is on the scene, if reluctantly, when Leonard is killed.

There are early signs in the story of the extremity to which the narrator will be reduced, not by any will of his own but by the dark, unrelenting energy of anti-Semitism and his need to respond outside the bounds of politeness or convention. As he looks at his own forebears, he has images of the tribal: "Cave-man talk, I would think, listening to the guttural sounds" of Hebrew. "We've all heard about those Russian Jews: semi-Cro-Magnon types covered in beards, furs, dense body hair, living without flush toilets or electricity in a post-feudal swamp of bone-breaking peasants, child-snatching witches, and wicked landowners." The style is jaunty here. You can hear a forced assumption of distance and superiority; the narrator and his family have passed "through the evolutionary gate of the twentieth century." But it isn't necessary to be a Jew to understand the ironies of E.J. Pratt's "From Stone to Steel":

> The snarl neanderthal is worn
> Close to the smiling Aryan lips,
> The civil polish of the horn
> Gleams from our praying finger tips.

What a long and a little way the race has come. "Racial Memories" climaxes with a savage moment, "one of those incidents that is not supposed to happen, a relic from other countries, other eras: just as Leonard was working himself to a climax [exercising his right to free speech in the enlightened new world], a policeman smashed his truncheon into the back of his head, sending him falling face forward onto the floor."

The aftermath of Leonard's death releases more than grief that might be assuaged by getting drunk with Peter, because more than an unlucky individual was lost. Leonard lived his life as a militant Jew and he died for his race, so his death was the death of a Jew, an outrage dense with racial memory of victimization. The narrator's conscious mind can't cope with the overwhelming understanding of how little has changed over the centuries, that there's never anywhere to hide, and his unconscious is even harder on him. He has a dream that ends by linking him, in bestial form, with a persecutor who is Leonard, also transformed by the dream: "When Leonard tries to arrest me I leap at his throat, bringing him to the ground and tearing at him until I wake myself up with my screams." Leonard *is* a sort of persecutor. As the inconvenient, ubiquitous, doubt-free conscience, he keeps the narrator in a Jewish slot he wants out of. Jewish identity will not accommodate all he wishes to be, but racist forces keep stuffing him back in there, so any breaking of ranks, even in thought, feels like betrayal. Identity crisis? An understatement.

In *Typing* Matt speaks only the once of "Racial Memories," but two other things in the book resonate with the last paragraph of the story. One is the description of himself as a "self-hating Jew," an appalling thing to see in print. The other is an episode out of his disillusionment with the "revolutionary" 1960s. Depressed, he visits a woman who had approached him on Toronto's hippy hangout, Yorkville Avenue. She "was into Buddhistic group therapy and costume jewellery," which doesn't sound promising, but she turns out to be a healer who can match Matt's shattered self with one of her own:

> I tried to explain that Ottawa Jews probably can't turn themselves into Toronto hippies. The term "Ottawa Jew" made her light a stick of incense and take out what she promised was some very special imported herbal tea. We sat on the porch and listened to sitar music while the light fell out of the

sky. When it was dark we went and lay down on her bed. Thanks to the special tea, her room had become a spaceship, her bed an enclosed platform in a rocket waiting to blast off to an undiscovered planet. We went into a black tunnel. At first it was the Tunnel of Endless Pleasure. Then it was simply a tunnel, simply pleasure, simply endless, simply black. I began to think that this was why "the young" read Nietzsche, that somewhere in this tightly wound spiral of pleasure, pain, infinite exhaustion and energy was where God must have died. Or dissolved in confusion.

Afterward she put on her sunglasses and made ordinary tea. "Naked woman with sunglasses," I said. She laughed. We drove through the city, the air moving through the leaves in a way it never would again. For the first time I had been with someone to whom some unspeakable violence had been done. What it was, I didn't know. Nor had she spoken of it. But it had left her a refugee, haunting the ruins of her own bombed-out city. She, I realized, was on the firm ground of suffering and pain accepted and overcome—ground that I could never know.

Not the particulars, maybe, but I think he found a parallel suffering in his own experience. I can't assume that "Racial Memories" is the story this adventure left Matt not yet "ready to write. Or even begin to think about," but "Racial Memories" does end in something very like it, a similar desperate, nonverbal intimacy. As the airport climax approaches, the story suddenly and exhilaratingly begins to snap in and out of the second person, the narrator addressing an unnamed "you," a stranger present at the airport protest and then at Leonard's funeral, after which she accompanies him to a hotel where almost all their communication is physical. Abandoned to their senses, they find a primitive release presented in language that might seem purple if the intensity of the story hadn't perfectly set up the scene and if it weren't metaphorically layering now with then, then being the story of Joseph Lucky, the "Jewish cowboy" and benefactor who travelled west by train and whose body, after death, was said to have been claimed by an "'unrecorded stranger.'" And the narrative itself is bunching up here, remembering at its close an unusually visceral marking of characters, by smell as well as appearance, and also the layering of the past in versions, historical and mythic, that are impossible to separate:

> Now this hotel is my train. You are my benefactress, wealthy in the dark cream skin that you inhabit, the mysterious odours of your mysterious places, your eyes that becalm everything they see. Under your protection we ride our wild animals into the twilight. Until beneath our starry blankets we find a way to sleep—out on the range, in this room which hovers in an otherwise unmarked universe, which exists for no other purpose than the mutual exploration of mutual desire. *Assimilated*, as Leonard used to say; against our non-existent will we have been assimilated into this compromised situation—two unrecorded strangers claiming each other with words sight touch smell until we raise spark enough to join our foreign bodies.

The promised land is a one-night stand, memorable but exceptional and temporary and mindless and so desperately sad.

Who is this man I've been calling "the narrator?" He's named after his great-great uncle, so he must be Joseph. His friends would probably call him Joe, but I can't. It would be presumptuous even to call him Joseph. If a reader were meant to tag him with a name, that name would be spoken in the story. "'You are the outsider,' Leonard is explaining to me, 'the perennial third man. You think it's because of your shiny metal mind. Forget it. You're outside because you're a Jew.'" Shiny metal mind? I doubt that a metal mind is given to agonizing and the narrator certainly is. He seems to be someone else to Leonard than he is to the reader. There is this one tantalizing hint of manufactured identity, perhaps that of an efficient lawyer. But the reticence is part of a motif. His father is the family "historian-in-exile, but that is another story." Why was the narrator, instead of his father, delegated to talk Laura out of marrying Peter Riley? "The explanation for this," he says, "lies in other stories, stories too long and intertwined to tell . . . , stories about my parents." The story that *is* told is incomplete, then. There's more to it, and maybe some of the more is being suppressed. Leonard's remark raises that suspicion. But, characteristically, he sees only half the picture. Equally detached from Jewishness, the narrator is a third man any way you look at him. A sense develops of essential anonymity, a self-effacement to be honoured in the uncertain, tortured identity of this man who renders the lives of others in such vivid particulars. It's not only the style of "Racial Memories" that speaks; so does the unspoken in the narrative point of view.

What would it have taken to show Matt's enlightened father, with his belief that "the study of arts was reserved for those whose brains and psyches were too feeble to tear off the blinders of superstition and ignorance," that "Racial Memories" is woven of the perennial struggle between enlightenment and ignorance, tolerance and savagery, right at the core of the human universe? If science was Dr. Cohen's Australian escape, forget it.

It can be tough enough to be a Jew without also having your purchase on life undermined by a withholding father. Either fate might have been enough to make Matt the cynic he claimed he was. At the end of *Typing* he is still writing of his "completely meaningless life." How much of that is rhetorical? How much is meant to draw a response like that of his "refugee" friend: "'You pretend to be a cynic. Really what you want is to believe in love. But you can't.'"

Nothing in *Typing* is either benevolent or sentimental. The past is painful and chaotic and the present is not mellow. Still, Matt's story is marked with epiphanies (the word is actually used) and it seems almost shapely in two respects. One is that *Elizabeth and After*, the novel Matt considers his best, "was obviously an inevitable point on the arc I'd seen so long ago when I began *The Disinherited*." The other is that the Matt who narrates this tale seems finally to believe in love. He acknowledges "the children, who along with Patsy and a few close friends have, through their ferocious loyalty and love, fashioned me a protective cloak that has made the impossible bearable." And he writes ardently about love in *Elizabeth and After*:

> There is so much to love. Cats. Bits of dust caught in the light. Colours. Unexpected waterfalls. And of course: the body. Warm skin on cool sheets. The

blood's night hum. Summer heat seeping through damp moss. The raw smell of an oak tree opened in winter. A long-missed voice over the telephone. So much to love that life should be made out of loving, so many ways of loving that all stories should be love stories.

Mavis Gallant was pleased to accept the new Writers' Trust Matt Cohen Prize for a body of writing because, like her, Matt Cohen was a writer and nothing but. I remember watching a CBC TV documentary about the difficult life of the Canadian writer. Matt was one of those featured. There he was, at his cabin during the winter, before the plumbing was hooked up, walking out across the snow to chop a hole in some ice and fill a pail with water. It felt a bit staged to dramatize the primitive conditions endured by Canadian writers, and it looked to me like Matt was enjoying the fiction of virtuous poverty he was helping to make for the Canadian viewing public. But he did work as a writer, for just about all of his adult life, in a time and place where it wasn't easy to make a living that way. If at some level Matt hoped that *Typing* might provoke the verdict that his life *was* meaningful, at least to others, I can easily oblige. He looked to me like a good husband and father. He was good company. I always admired his dedication, his discipline, and I admire it more now, thinking that the man who wrote his MA thesis on the political thought of Albert Camus might well have identified with Camus's *The Myth of Sisyphus* which "poses mortal problems" but "sums itself up for me as a lucid invitation to live and to create, in the very midst of the desert." In my company, Matt never seemed to be writhing in that desert, and I realize that the *Typing* I've been taking so seriously has its light side, but together with his fiction it stresses loneliness, abandonment, the absence of any system to live by. There's something Sisyphean to producing twenty-five books in thirty-one years (not counting the pseudonymous and ghost-written) without any faith to depend on.

The Governor General's medal for *Elizabeth and After* doesn't figure in *Typing*, and I don't quite know what to make of it myself. It does add an exclamation to the point at the end of that arc of completion, but not without irony. If the medal were some sort of climax to the story of a writer's life, what about the dénouement? It should have turned into another arc. But for those who like closure, loose ends tied up, *Typing* delivers. The book was written in the five months after Matt was diagnosed with terminal cancer. In that time he also wrote the two stories needed to finish *Getting Lucky*, and pushed his novel about Joseph Roth into a favourite phase of creation, "the slow and always surprising discovery of its particular universe, with its language, its people, its cities and countryside." He almost got it all done in what would have been a remarkable five months in the life of a healthy man.

&

it was terribly hot and muggy in June of 1980, the kind of Ontario summer weather that gives CBC Toronto conniptions about killer smog & keeps announcers urging seniors not to leave their air-conditioned homes. At his eastern Ontario cabin, Matt went out for a walk with his spaniel Teddy & their guest Paddy, an Irish Wolfhound. Matt was boarding Paddy while the Moss family travelled in England. He was the size of a yearling calf & quite playful, not being very old even in dog years, but his heart gave out on the path that day & he died. Matt may have been sorry for Paddy & sorry for the bereaved travellers, but it wasn't long before he saw the humour in being lumbered with a great big shaggy stiff whose long legs he hadn't thought to fold up ahead of rigor mortis. The country north of Kingston is as unforgivingly rocky & rootbound as Al Purdy's Country North of Belleville, you see, & Matt's property has a lot of bush on it. Even the big hardwoods root mostly in swamp or rock. No wonder some of them blow right down in a big wind. You could have trouble finding a good place to bury even a small dog, & it might be a struggle even with the proper tools. Matt was a writer, not a farmer.

So he phoned Steve Jones, who was working on his '54 GMC truck at Blue Roof Farm that summer. Steve drove over with a pickaxe and a couple of shovels & together he and Matt sweated for the rest of the day to stuff poor Paddy into the ground.

Matt enjoyed telling that story—at his cabin on the very day of the events, I think. I seem to remember Steve smiling a bit doubtfully as it unfolded, & I see lemonades that he and Matt needed more than we did. Lemonades slide into the story where I would expect beers, so it's clearly blurred at the edges. I don't know if Matt kept the story in a bag of anecdotes to be opened every so often, but I did. An aversion to name-dropping always kept Matt out of the narrative—"A friend," I'd begin, or "A fellow I know was taking care of a dog one time." Re-telling has kept the core of the story fresh. If I were a real & not a reluctant storyteller, I might possess an entire oral history. I might have a lot more to say about Matt, all of it sharp.

I wrote Matt when I heard he was dying. In his reply he said he wished he'd be around to hear all about Newfoundland. He'd have loved Mercedes Barry's story about her great-grandfather on Merasheen Island. A small, wiry man, he made the mistake of teasing a large billy goat. The goat charged, impaled its tormentor, then ran spooked all over the island with the corpse stuck on his horns, community pursuit much hampered by laughter.

Mydra Ellen Dragland
1914–1998

Hortus Conclusus

All week we were looking over the wall from Corpus Christi College down into Christ Church gardens. One afternoon there were two-dimensional gardeners down there, very like playing cards whenever they turned side-on, and on another day we saw two people rather self-consciously playing croquet with flamingo mallets and hedgehog balls. Later, I saw the long-necked brass fire dogs, one each side of the fireplace in Christ Church Great Hall, that Lewis Carroll borrowed for Alice, her neck "opening out like the largest telescope that ever was! Goodbye feet!" There was only one fireplace in that huge hall with its stained glass windows, hung with portraits of famous men of the House. On winter days you'd want to be dining damn close to that fire.

The walled gardens of Christ Church. Well, most of the old Oxford Colleges are walled. All over the city centre, the walls are partly composed of buildings, so the life of the mind is in the walls. That's where the people are, the students and the dons and the porters and the professors. And now, at Easter break, all of us conference-goers have gathered from the fringes and beyond the fringes of empire. We're all in the walls of Corpus Christi College: the dining hall, the junior common room, the seminar rooms, the residence rooms, the rathskellar pub beneath the dining hall. Gathered by the British Council into this ancient centre of learning for the purpose of perpetuating English literature and British culture unto the ends of the earth, yea, even in 1995.

There wasn't a single discussion all week—not one—about this suck of the British centre. Britons, certain that Oxford could hold us nicely, that we were privileged to be here, gave the matter no thought. The rest of us never discussed it. We simply carried our own centres with us and introduced them to each other. Mine, invisible in the official sessions—nary a Canadian poet referred to—surfaced in conversations with Gemino from the Phillipines, Anette from East Germany, and Anne Margarethe from Denmark. Vladislava thought I ought to attend the conference on "Beginnings in Canadian Literature" in Yugoslavia that May. Amazing, such a perceptive theme for a conference on the literature of my country in a country that was disintegrating.

As a boy in Manila, Gemino—"Jerry" since studying for his PhD in California—saw all the Western movies he could. He always rooted for the Indians. I gave him a copy of *Floating Voice*, my book that also roots for the Indians, and he gave me his poems. A good swap. I loved the way his face opened and his whole body rose up to greet anything he liked, a word, a person. I've never felt such a thrill hearing a man say my name: Stan, a word full of meaning in his voice.

"A Green Treasure of Europe" says the brochure about Slovenia that Uros gave me. Slovenia looked wonderful in the pictures, but then I had already fallen for the Slovenians, Uros and Milena. How to understand these affinities? That man in Jammu—his name is lost, as is wherever in India he came from, but our intimacy is not, our sharing of confidences within moments of meeting. Ancient friends, you'd think. His gift to me was offering himself whole and expecting no less in return. Uros and Milena were more like the usual me: reserved. Handshakes rather than hugs when we said goodbye.

Waiting for the taxi, I asked Uros what his name meant.

It's from the Latin, *ursus*, he said.

Bear.

Yes.

For Milena I was turning over some names of my own. Milena Wall Climber? Milena Wall Walker? She'd stood out for me even before her great escape from Christ Church gardens—locked in after closing time—but after! I was half joking, offering to write her up, as we waited outside Corpus Christi. Myth, realism? I gave her a choice. She wasn't having it, still embarrassed at the way she'd crashed back into the conference, but then I asked right out, what if I write about you, and she hesitated. Well, she said finally, it's okay.

You see, said Uros, smiling, with a tone just this side of triumphant that revealed much about them both. Milena will act before she'll speak but even self-effacing Milena is not entirely without vanity and even generous-minded Uros notes that smugly.

◄o►

I didn't really want to look down into those Christ Church Gardens where Milena found herself locked in; I didn't want to look down there and think England, Empire—all gothic and foursquare and closed like the minds of the nice British professors, not Oxford professors, who were squiring us though this week-long celebration of British poetry. "Trendy," they complained about any unorthodox presentation; "Flavour of the month," they called anything that threatened to open a gate in their heads. Between those untasting minds and those gardens—the huge chestnut that knew Charles Dodgson and Alice Liddell—what necessary connection? No connection, none. At least not until Milena got locked in there.

One of the nice professors complained to me that someone had complained to him about the lack of theory at the conference. "What does she expect?" he spat, and I expected him to continue, "Flavour of the month, probably," but he missed the chance. There were few tough questions being asked, and the few independent questioners could be safely cut down over a pint at The Mitre or The Bear. Spooked by theory deep in an age of theory. After my paper Milena mentioned the shortage of theory, and I realized that the malcontent was her. But she wasn't interested in the trendy. She emanated curiosity and she saw theory where others might not. I'd quoted Robert Bringhurst ("the *made form* of poetry is only the audible half of the conversation"), arguing that creative writing makes good readers. "Once written, twice read," she translated for me out of Slovenian.

—◄O►—

Milena stands at the south gate of Christ Church College, looking out through the bars at Christ Church Meadow, just after five on a Thursday afternoon. Her chin is in her hand because the bowler-hatted porters have locked up and gone home and left her inside.

That walled garden is not the British mind. Of course not. It certainly isn't the brilliant mind of Valentine Cunningham of Corpus Christi College who addressed us on the making of a new anthology of nineteenth-century British poetry. Still, it's especially important to me that Milena gets out of there, more so than if it were just any old garden with standard playing-card gardeners and croquet players with avian mallets. So I wish I'd asked her how she did it. Technique is always interesting.

I see Milena choosing the likeliest wall—the one on the Corpus Christi side where, if she shouted, one of us might look over the edge and, what, reach down? It's a long way down, at least ten feet. No, someone would have to hang over the edge, a Bangladeshi, say, with a Belgian to the left leg and a Malaysian to the right. Jump now, grab my arms. Kaiser's Bangladeshi chin would have scraped the stones, but he would have worn his bruise with pride, just as he wore the full moustache that Gyözo declared was Hungarian, at which the rest of us at the banquet table declared ourselves Hungarian too. I could just glimpse in Gyözo what melancholy we would all be masking with sardonic smiles if *Hungarian* should happen to stick.

Or else a Dane down over the edge, with a Russian and a Swiss to hold his legs—Mark, for example. He's more bear than Uros. Tall and broad, a triathlete, someone said. He never came though a door without crashing some part of his body into the frame. There is help available from every far-flung centre-fringe imaginable. But no. Milena wants out of Christ Church Garden without causing any fuss.

Now I have to stand with chin in hand and think with you, Milena. I have to walk over and inspect the wall on the Corpus Christi side. Across that beautiful lawn, manicured as for cricket, and into the shrubs at the perimeter. We need a spot with a gap between shrubs. Good thing it's only April and this English garden is not in full bloom. A gap, yes, here beside this cascading forsythia (pronounced with a long *i* by the English), because we can't get up that wall by leaping over shrubs. The wall is rough right here. That's good. Rocks protrude from the masonry because this is a piece of the original city wall left after Cromwell's soldiers broke up the rest in 1646.

Okay. Now fifteen paces back and turn. Measure the top like the jumpers we once were. Mark the middle of the wall. We have to get one foot up that high. Right? Now draw a deep breath, rear back, start our run. Over the grass past the shrubbery up! Yes! The right foot finds a ledge, the leg straightens. Two hands over the top, now the other foot, the knee—that smarts!—an elbow finds purchase and then! Uros looks up from flicking away a butt, his eyes widening in astonishment, as Milena drops into Corpus Christi College from the Christ Church side.

How did you do it without beating up your knees, your hands, your shoes? I saw no lacerations, no scuffing. You're amazing, Milena. You don't want attention. You went over the wall to get over the wall. You want to be remarked, if at all, as nowt but a tall ghost on the video record at the barred gate where you briefly stood with chin in hand, pondering. I believe you can do anything, Milena. Milena Wall Walker, Milena Up And Over. First place in the wall vault, Oxford Olympics, 1995.

Slovenian national anthem, please.

&

at every session of the conference a wiry, intense man would feature in the question period. I have two questions, he always began. & why not? His questions were always good ones. But eventually one of our kind hosts frostily slapped him down. One question per questioner would, he felt, be quite enough. Some of us, the implication was, were getting more than our proper share. I'd have given up one of my questions. I hadn't asked any & thus had a backlog. I have two questions, we might then have heard, one of my own & one in proxy for that bearded gentleman sitting near the wall. Eyes would swing to me, & I'd nod, confirming. It's not so easy to slap down a movement that may be forming, especially when widely scattered parts of the quondam empiah unite in it.

I passed the questioner in the residence hallway that evening. I think they're on to you, I said. I don't remember if he answered. I don't remember a smile. He was a *very* intense man. Perhaps he'd felt humiliated. A long way from India, he was in the familiar country of Shakespeare, the foreign country of appalling dot-bangers—skinheads who attack any woman they see with a bindi.

I heard about dot-bangers in Kolkata—but that's leaping ahead of my invitation to speak there by this same avid questioner, who turned out to be Professor Subir Dhar of Rabindra Bharati University, Kolkata, Blake scholar & secretary of the Shakespeare Society of Eastern India, leaping ahead of his extraordinary response to my paper. In solidarity, when I finished reading it, I was going to invite him to ask me two questions, but there was just time to deliver the paper before we all had to rush off to the next plenary session. After which he approached me.

Indians are emotional people, he said of his open-hearted welcome of my words, but this is not that. He must have assumed that I would discount an emotional response. This was our first real contact, so he couldn't know how often I'd sat in the classrooms & conference rooms of my own university, an undemonstrative Canadian, listening in aesthetic transport to my colleague, Balachandra Rajan—not an emotional Indian, so far as I could tell—hearing him raise & raise & raise the bar of thinking in beautiful, powerful prose. Subir couldn't know how well I understood what he was saying, how my own heart rose to it because I never expected to hear such a thing addressed to me. In England, by a man from India?

You never know. Since you don't, there are surprises. Some of the surprises beat you down, but this was sure not that. No indeed. & so an ancient world, new to me, was opened up.

India.

Kolkata, Dibrugarh, Varanasi. Then, a year later, Jammu, New Delhi, Agra.

Am I the daughter you always wanted, Rachel asks, & yes, we say, yes, always yes. You're the one. You're the very daughter we wanted, the best daughter in the whole wide world. & Toby and Simon are the best sons, right? They are the best. They're the very sons we always wanted. My love, we couldn't be luckier. Her smile of pleasure so beautiful & natural it breaks my heart to think how easily she might lose it, the smile & the pleasure. Wishing her a gentle voyage, knowing it's wrong to want for her a life of lullaby. Wynken, Blynken & Nod. Well, it's not going to happen. My love.

Subir—is he the listener I always wanted? The total stranger who hears my words & knows me instantly? I don't know how to answer except with the climax, the parade scene, of Michael Ondaatje's *Coming Through Slaughter*. Buddy Bolden didn't know what he wanted for his music either, not until he saw it. Saw *her*. "You learn to play like that," Crawley had told him—like weather, volatile, like conversation, snatches of a crowd you move through, hard kiss on the mouthpiece, like a, damn, like a goat hopped in the front seat of your Volks, like a new $7.50 ring would, right, it would save your marriage, like a mountain railroad, yodel, like a black snake on your deck, like three old ladies locked in a lavatory, like blood, like stains, like blood blood heart blood air, exactly the tone of this room—"play like that and no band will play with you."

Crawley was another cornet. He'd been a friend. So he drops away behind. There are grooves he knows how to go in.

&, no, Buddy is not in the best of shape. His brain suicided. Something cutting away all that binds him to others. Something in that razor edge he needs. No, we understand this well enough to stand back, a little apart from Crawley (except to whisper, "*If you break* my love *break going out not in*"). After all his privacy of practice, Buddy is just about to get it right. But "no *band* will play with you?" That's putting it mildly. Who'll be his friend at that ether altitude, long after the parade, if not for the unjudging sun?

But right now his cornet's a-honk, squawking, snarling, & "where the bitch came from I don't know. She moves out to us again, moving along with us, gravy bones. Thin body and long hair and joined by someone half bald and a beautiful dancer too so I turn from the bank of people and aim at them and pull them on a string to me, the roar at the back of my ears." Well, world on a string, he's got them sometimes. Sometimes she has him. "*Roar.* It comes back now, so I can hear only in waves now and then, god the heat in the air, she is sliding round and round her thin hands snake up through her hair and do their own dance and she is seven foot tall with them and I aim at them to bring them down to my body and the music gets caught in her hair, this is what I wanted, always, loss of privacy in the playing, leaving the stage, the rectangle of band on the street, this hearer who can throw me in the direction and the speed she wishes like an angry shadow."

& shortly "his mind on the pinnacle of something collapsed" & so far as the music is concerned that is that. Silver reaches. Where two or three have won. Leaving the likes of Crawley and Prose Cornish to count the cost. & all of what's lost just has to be—accepted? But listen. There's still a rat's voice, small, still a small sly meanness spilt over from incomprehension: "Laughing in my room. As you try to explain me I will spit you, yellow, out of my mouth." You talkina me? Hawked gob. You talkina *me*? Right up to there I was thinking that's that. But you prick, you, calling me to step up over those other bodies! *What is it?* Root, I'll explain you in a dance, blossom & bole. Stiff Canadian, watch me now, my shoulders back like as if my dad was alongside, proudly south down the streets of muses, my shirt as red as yours if it comes to that, you asshole, in the Horseshoe Tavern, & just about Iberville I'm stepping out limber into my strut. When the Saints. Rat Bite. A Closer Walk with Thee.

    What I want?

R

Transit

> I am the tourist. I am the prodigal who hates the foreigner.
>
> Michael Ondaatje, *Running in the Family*

The evenings were cold in Jammu that January. It was colder, coldest for the January travellers from the north who were expecting subcontinental warmth. The spectacular view of the Himalayas from Air India windows recalled the effect of elevation on climate but it was too late. Travellers to the conference from other parts of India had brought scarves, heavy jackets, fur hats; our winter clothes were back in Canada.

At the end of the first day of presentations, the promised car did not appear to return chilled Canadians to their heated hotel. We stood about shivering, some of us more annoyed than I thought seemly. Our hosts ushered us up to a brazier of coals some workers had lit to warm themselves. I didn't think that was right either. Professor Malhotra had an idea. Would you like a drink, he asked. I have some rum in my room. Sounds good, I replied, and he left us.

Returning, he showed us into a seminar room off the courtyard of the humanities building. There were four glasses of rum and water on the table. Seeing that, my colleagues recoiled. Outside of a movie, I had never seen actual recoiling. They mumbled their thanks-but-no-thanks and returned to the brazier. I couldn't blame them; only I had anything invested in the moment, since the kind offer had been made through me. And I couldn't accept either, having once lost two days in Kolkata to some dietary indiscretion that I still don't understand. I explained that our delicate Canadian innards could not risk Indian water, but there was no bridging the awkwardness.

Later in the evening, now warmed by an excellent dinner, I ran into Professor Malhotra. He had not let the rum go to waste. He was unsteady and there was food on his chin. He could not keep his pain from showing. I failed, he said.

In my own country I am socially inept. An overdeveloped sense of irony and an undeveloped sense of when to use it combine to keep me admiring graciousness from afar. But in India it is said that the guest is a god, and story after story is told to reinforce the lesson. Temporary god that I was, I had no need of irony. It is completely impossible to fail, I said to Professor Malhotra, in a gesture of genuine hospitality. My words may have been appropriate for once, but they had no effect. He was inconsolable.

—◄o►—

This man held up a worn paperback copy of Margaret Atwood's *Surfacing*. He could not understand certain passages in the novel, he said. Would I be so good as to tell him what they were about. Each of the three problem passages he showed me was an indented quotation. Two of the quotations were from children's rhymes. One of these also appears in Robert Kroetsch's "Seed Catalogue," where it lower-cases the myth of the fall:

> Adam and Eve and Pinch Me
> Went to the river to bathe;

> Adam and Eve fell in,
> So who do you think was saved?

Scarcely a Canadian kid has failed to learn from this rhyme how viciously a proper noun may turn into an imperative sentence. This is why so few in my country enjoy ambiguity. It was pinched out of us when we were kids.

The other passage was from the singing of Vera Lynn:

> There'll be bluebirds over
> The white cliffs of Dover
> Tomorrow, when the world is free . . .

I'm a generation and an ocean removed from those who hoped their way through World War II with the help of that song, but I know what it meant to them and so I know what it means, or rather what it is doing, in Atwood's book.

Since I can identify those passages, I could start with any of them and work my way into *Surfacing* or out into the culture the novel comes from. Since my Indian friend had no purchase on those rhymes, they were blanks in a text that must elsewhere have been closed to him as well. He was immensely grateful for annotations that cost me nothing. As for me, I had travelled all the way to India to be shown three passages in *Surfacing* that had been invisible to me. I had never paid attention to them. My new friend was too distant and I too near. Together, we shared a pair of eyes.

I am grateful for much more than the new perspective on *Surfacing* given me by a man willing to hazard simple questions. There can hardly be enough reminders that ignorance hides in knowledge. Strangeness lurks in the familiar reality I sleepwalk through every day. If I were to wake? Amazing Grace. I once was blind, but now I see.

―◄o►―

There is a Borges story, "Averroës' Search," about a translator of Aristotle who is "nonplussed by two equivocal words at the beginning of the *Poetics*: the words *tragedy* and *comedy*. . . . No one within the compass of Islam intuited what they meant." Sealed within his own rich culture, and confident that Islam encompasses reality, Averroës has no choice but to find Islamic equivalents for foreign terms. He broods and broods about Aristotle's words until, after an evening of wine and collegial disputation in which his orthodoxy has shone most brilliantly, it suddenly comes to him what Aristotle's words must mean. The solution to his problem, Englished from the Spanish of Borges by Anthony Kerrigan, is as follows: "*Aristu (Aristotle) calls panegyrics by the name of tragedy and anathemas he calls comedies. The Koran abounds in remarkable tragedies, and so do the Mohalacas of the Sanctuary.*" Averroës is missing the boat by weeks.

At this point in the story, the scholar and his milieu that Borges had worded so painstakingly, "suddenly, as if fulminated by a bolt of flameless fire," poof! disappears. The surprise ending seems both weird and unfair until Borges folds it back on himself. The fiction of Averroës having exploded, the irony suddenly doubles as the narrator removes his omniscient mask and confesses as author: "I sensed that Averroës, striving to imagine what a drama is without ever having suspected what a theatre was, was no more absurd than I, who strove to imagine Averroës with no material other than some fragments from Renan, Lane and Asín Palacios." The fiction evaporates when the author stops believing in it.

My encounter in India changed this story for me. Now I am inside it, as both the blind Averroës and "Borges" the self-reflexive writer, and I am outside it as well—outside with my irony on hold, admiring the writer who travels so far and so ardently from his desk and then abruptly, in an onset of humility, scraps a creation he had made me believe in. Having risked another reality, though, he is not absurd. Blessed are those who see their own culture circumscribed.

◄o►

If he loves the landscape he enters, does the foreigner cease to be a tourist?

&

Spanner/Wrench

immigrant: "over here my friends think me ludicrously filial, whereas over there i'm considered barely filial. over there, they think me lazy & naive, whereas over here, some think me sagely & epigrammatic. a friend from here who went back there with me observed that those traits of mine which drove her crazy (my punctiliousness, aloneness, hardness, sense of duty) are casual! when compared to my family. there, i'm deemed too relaxed, here i'm reckoned too goal-oriented. over here, people complain i'm curt on the phone, over there, they wonder why i waste time giving out details . . . "

local: "so what do you do with all this??"

immigrant: "i . . . span it."

jam. ismail

S

Sufficient Elasticity

> The loon pours into its dive like
> water into water,
> heart—breaking call —
> in my mouth.

Is truth beauty?
It could be.

Truth could still be beauty if
(tendering the words) you love
whatever you have made of them.

> It could still be the case
> that "Beauty is truth, truth beauty."

> That could still be "all/ ye know on earth,
> and all ye need to know."
>
> Accepting the hyperbole with one muscle of your love, loving the rhetoric so, you could still believe a sphere of knowledge and experience rounded between the two words. As the register of world and word slides in and out of true. Phantom meaning. Ask the peg-leg Sea Cook what is and isn't there.

Crazy as a loon
they say, and that's true too—
laughing that haywire yodel and
slap slap slap slap slap slap slap slap slapping wingtips to
water, needing, *look*, the whole damn lake for a takeoff run—
    even if *la lune*
    is what they mean.

&

jus d'orange?

Reading that, I'd get it. But I haven't heard any French words spoken for ages, not to me. In London, Ontario, nobody ever addresses me in French. So I'm out of practice. I'm out of my element at the counter of this hotel restaurant in Montreal. Breakfast is included & I've presented myself for breakfast. *Petit déjeuner*, why didn't he start with that? I'd have recognized that. As it is, I'm just seconds away from understanding, as the tumblers roll & roll, processing (*jeu, jou, je vous . . . d'érange, dérange? Vous me dérange? You're making me crazy? Monsieur, pourquoi?*), when

Orange juice?

Oui, merci. Which I suppose means nothing to him but Yes, thanks.

A small humiliation. Linguistically inept in my "own" country.

& I told that one on myself for years before I started wondering, pourquoi jus d'orange et aucune d'autre? Pourquoi pas jus de tomate, jus de pomme, jus de pamplemousse? Orange juice was & is fine, merci beaucoup, but a range of words of the same species would be an arrow saying "you are here."

Spanner

The word "bridge," in the name of the Alberta city on the banks of the Belly River that was named for William Lethbridge, no longer signifies.

But there is one helluva bridge in that city. Here is a postcard of it. On the reverse, under the space for a message, is the caption: "The longest, highest railroad bridge of its kind in the world. Constructed in 1909 in Lethbridge, Alberta." I bought the postcard to take into my classes whenever I taught Thomas King's *Medicine River*. Harlan Bigbear tricks his brother Joe into jumping off that bridge, and young Lum is a suicide off that bridge, or one like it, in King's *Truth & Bright Water*. The same bridge is the key to my past, and a clue to my moving now.

My father had a small stock of family stories, like the one about my jumping into the Banff Hotsprings pool at the age of six. I had never been near a pool but swimming looked simple from the observation deck above, so I hustled into my trunks and raced from the change room to the pool and jumped in at the five-foot level. The second time I surfaced, someone noticed and pulled me out by the hair. The punch line my father savoured was the line I met him with as he emerged poolside: Dad!—he always caught the amazement in my tone—I can't swim at all!

And my father used to tell about hopping a freight in the dirty thirties on the Lethbridge side of the world's longest and highest bridge and hanging in numb terror out over the valley until the train made the far side and he tumbled off, never to ride the rails again. So I was conceived out west, in Alberta. I was not and never will be born in Ontario, where I lived the second half of my life to date, where my children were born. Two thousand miles away from Alberta and that bridge back in Lethbridge, an okay place to visit but you wouldn't want to live there. Don't have to; I brought Alberta with me when I moved east. And sometimes, during one of those long, lovely Ontario evenings, if I'm not careful, having had one too many Scotches, I feel Alberta begin to throb inside me and I hear some ambient western movie soundtrack stir, and start to swell and, and (wouldn't you know it) there's my dad's beautiful tenor in unison with the Yodelling Cowboy, Wilf Carter:

> In the Blue Canadian Rockies
> Spring is sighing through the trees . . .

◂○▸

Look at all the bad that happens when the favourite daughter refuses to say what she feels for the king, her father. But how could she be direct without occupying the low ground her false sisters have claimed? "I love you as meat loves salt," she says, and the old fool flies into a rage. There *is* no story if he catches the wink of travel between what she says and what she means, I realize that. And nothing will stop these stories from happening. Nobody solves the riddle before riding to hell and back. But I can't help thinking that a literary education would have done this father some good—a course in narrative patterns might have been helpful, but I'm especially thinking of rhetoric. If the field marks of trope had been explained to him, for example, he might have read his daughter aright. There's no crossing those tiny bridges of metaphor when you come to them if you can't even *see* them.

—◄o►—

Duncan Campbell Scott had been best friends with Pelham Edgar for almost fifty years when he wrote to a relative that "Edgar is here now in the Censors and is rather a thorn in our flesh. Between ourselves, one gets impatient with an old friend sometimes who has not learned, after all these years, to understand one's likes and dislikes and who keeps rubbing one's fur in the wrong direction so often." Too bad, this static between old buddies, but my mind slides off it to the vision of a man becoming a cat before my very eyes. It was natural enough for Scott, who confessed that he was addicted to cats (he always wrote with a cat across his knees) and who quite approved of Mark Twain's habit of renting a few cats to prowl the hotel room wherever he was on tour. Yes, that is Scott's cat Skookum frolicking on the music-room floor with Rupert Brooke in 1913 while Scott, smoothing his whiskers, watches. There doesn't seem to be a human anywhere in the Lisgar Street house tonight, but there will be. Just wait until flame-haired Belle gets home. Brooke wrote to Harold Munro back in England that Scott was "the only poet in Canada" and "a nice fellow." "He has a wife," Brooke added, period. Nuff said between old boys and cat fanciers. Reading "wife," the hairs stood up at the back of Munro's neck.

Maybe it's silly, maybe it's sentimental, to gravitate towards those critics whose reading practice agrees with yours, but wouldn't it be perverse not to? Would you choose your friends out of those who rub your fur the wrong way? Maybe you would, maybe you should. It's very easy to get too comfortable while reading, dozing in front of the fire after dinner with paws tucked in. Maybe you need a reveille. Maybe you need a dose of my colleague, Frank Davey. Maybe *I* do, that is. Frank is from Abbotsford, British Columbia, but he writes as if he were from Missouri, the "Show Me" state. "I am myself," he says in *Post-National Arguments*, "conflicted in particular ways that have the potential to alienate me in some way . . . from elements in nearly every Canadian text which I encounter." Reading across the grain, he raises a profile of text that shows itself to no other approach, so it would be folly not to pay attention.

That car at the end of *In the Skin of a Lion*, for instance: Hana and Patrick are taking it to Marmora where Clara awaits them. Frank wonders how "a sixteen-year-old orphan and a labourer newly released from jail" could "acquire it late in the Canadian Depression?" That they can, he says "speaks volumes about the text's preference for art over history, economics, and cultural contest." An interesting point. Has he got the goods on the novel, then: it's not the radical text it pretends to be? No, not when so much in the elliptical narrative is left to the reader, including what to make of the politics in it. I could figure out where that car came from if I felt the need to put my mind to it, thus shrinking all those volumes into a footnote.

Frank's criticism often rubs me the wrong way. I turn from his distance, his resistance, to the truest thing Duncan Campbell Scott ever said in prose: "efforts [of criticism] to define what is undefinable inevitably tend to become creative attempts, approximate to poetic utterance, and endeavour to capture the spirit of poetry by luring it with a semblance of itself."

◂○▸

I feel so lonesome facing the flood of 19—. That road is washed out—so much water on the prairie, the prairie so flat the water spreads and spreads. Lake Agassiz. You only learn later where you were. There is a sepia photo. A father in a rumpled suit—he has been driving in the suit. Why would he not at least remove his jacket in the heat? A suit and a fedora. The sweat from his brow has soiled the felt above the sweat band. Most of this is not visible in the photo. He stands, and his wife stands beside him, looking into the flood. There is a child in his arms and though that child is a girl with bobbed hair, she is also me, as I am also—thanks to my Ontario distance—this camera/man seeing and saying to you what I see. Having flown across the ocean to do so in Germany. And when I return to Canada it will not be to my second home in Ontario but to a Newfoundland whose songs and stories and jokes travelled west and began to make a Newfoundland inside me. But that couple—forlorn—with their forlorn child, they had hoped for something new in these bad, dry years. There was news of land north of that now-uncrossable water where they could homestead, land the government would give them just for improving it. Now the future is drowned.

Say what you like. Say what the textbooks tell about Lake Agassiz, how it covered the prairie after the last ice age. Say anything you want, it's still not right that so much hope should be dashed in 19— by a flood that dried up millennia ago. Those people had drifted for years like prairie topsoil in the wind, and now they were going home to a land that had drowned. It just isn't right.

&

> [M]y theory of technique,if I have one, is very far from original; nor is it complicated. I can express it in fifteen words,by quoting The Eternal Question And Immortal Answer of burlesk, viz. "Would you hit a woman with a child?—No,I'd hit her with a brick" Like the burlesk comedian, I am abnormally fond of that precision which creates movement.
>
> e.e. cummings

Liselotte was driving me to lunch at the humanities building on Königsworther Platz. We were talking about school reunions. At Liselotte's reunion everyone had defined themselves by where their parents were now, dead or alive, thriving or no. There was another reason the experience had been depressing: after all those years, no one had changed a tittle. Which made me think of Andrew Corkish.

At registration in the Oyen Legion Hall, there he was, same old Corky, except wasn't he thinner somehow? Why was I looking up instead of straight across at him? That's right, he said, beaming, you haven't seen me for twenty years. I grew some. Some! A post-secondary growth spurt of twelve inches? And his basketball career behind him!

I said to Liselotte that graduates of Oyen High (eleven of us in my year) seemed to have stayed pretty much the same, though it was hard to tell, & there were some surprises. Alvin Furneaux owned a small airline in northern Alberta. That was hard to credit, seeing that he had never been able to execute a proper hook shot. Glenn Kenny had his own plane, but then he'd taken over the farm right after graduation. No surprise there. Glenn flew to Kindersley & picked up Kentucky Fried Chicken for the banquet on Saturday. A few years later he had a heart attack in the air & lived to write about it for a flying magazine my sister sent me. But oddest of all, I said to Liselotte, was this guy Andrew Corkish who'd grown a foot.

Her mouth dropped open, & I could see her face struggling not to register disbelief. For a second I couldn't think why.

Then I saw what she was seeing: Corky's extra foot, shoeless and sockless, the toes wiggling. The foot sticking out of his stomach. The oyster & the clam must now be his kin. Gastropod: an animal of the *Gasteropoda* class or group of molluscs, so called from the ventral position of the locomotive organ.

If it had been me driving, I'd have had to pull over, gasping, my eyes full of tears. Liselotte was laughing too, but with less abandon. Good thing; Leibnizstrasse was no joke. She must have been thinking, out of metric, about the word. Foot: I, 1 the lowest part of the leg beyond the ankle joint; III, 7 a lineal measure, originally based on the length of a man's foot.

Liselotte recovered first. The language will do that, she said, meaning it splits without warning. Meaning makes room for other meaning. The word healing itself. An appendage, a measure (of distance, of verse), once they were one.

U

Elpenor

> Ye'll tak the high road
> An I'll tak the low road
>> Lady John Scott

Théa Gray sends me her personal anthology of Canadian poetry, poems and passages from the red heart on her sleeve, copied out in her own careful hand and, when necessary, improved. The covering letter has a PS: "Why don't you write about Elpenor?" Théa knows that I like Elpenor best of all the minor characters in *The Odyssey*: Elpenor and Argos, the faithful dog who rises from the dung heap to greet Odysseus in Ithaca twenty years later. Humans are easier to fool than dogs. No disguise could fool a dog.

Which of the companions goes with Odysseus to the underworld? None. At least that's the idea. Odysseus is to go on his own and everybody else to hang around until he gets back. And no activities laid on. Boring. So some of the boys get up to no good, and suddenly Elpenor is a traveller, none swifter, none more reluctant. One minute he was walking the roof-beam at Circe's—got a snootfull of the wild wine and somebody dared him—the next minute he was dead. Odysseus of many wiles took ages to reach the underworld. If he had set one foot down wrong on the way there, if he had skipped one step out of Circe's elaborate directions, it would have been back to square one. Or worse—remember that bagful of wind? I suppose Elpenor was one of those who got suspicious and wanted a look inside.

Whoosh!

Why couldn't Odysseus ever confide in somebody? See what happens when you hoard information?

Elpenor, they were laughing at you right up until your foot slipped. Why is it you, least of all the companions of resourceful Odysseus, who has become a name for always wandering with a hungry heart—why is it you I love the most?

Elpenor, you are never coming home.

Better to gasp once into a breaking wave and be swept away than eke out an easy life on land that tamely supports you. Doesn't the heart lift to that kind of thing? Doesn't it just inflate you with the kind of conviction that soldiers plain people into battle for the grand cause? Where they are mowed down by the other side. Before the "battle" of Beaumont Hamel, July 1, 1916, the Newfoundland Regiment numbered 801. Only sixty-eight answered to their names at roll-call next day. It took the Germans less than half an hour to do that. Somebody in command didn't think it all the way through. For the High Muckamucks, "casualty" was nothing but a casual word.

Elpenor, casualty of wild wine and evil will, return to Ithaca was never in the cards for you. Would you have preferred a hero's plunge into that breaking wave and drowning in the Earth Shaker to your own slightly comic fate? I think not. After all, every other one of the lost companions died the death of an extra. You alone were granted a voice. In a story rich with stories and tellers it means something to narrate your own death, even if the tale is nothing but climax.

—◄o►—

There was this big party at the apartment on Johnston Street where all the real parties seemed to happen that year. This was 1969, Elpenor, the end of the turbulent 1960s, and the students gathered in that second-storey apartment on Johnston St. in Kingston, Ontario, were doing their best to get loaded on the wild wine—those who weren't smoking up—or the barley brew. Here's the part you'll like:

The beer had filled my bladder to the overflow, and the john was occupied, so I stepped out onto the unlit rear balcony and started down the fire-escape, looking for a dark place to relieve myself. The stairs turned left from the landing but I turned right and stepped into a gap between landing and wall. I plunged five or six feet down, twisting, my back scraping brick. My right foot remained hooked on the landing. Those were my flexible days, Elpenor, and a drunk, as you know, is extra pliable. I ended up locked in a high kick.

You, Elpenor: one false step and your neck bone is snapped.

Me, I couldn't just walk away from that drop with one leg hiked up over my head, but I couldn't stop laughing either.

Now here's the thing, Elpenor: if the apartment had been on the fifth floor, or the sixth, I would have turned in the wrong direction, and I would have dropped right into Hades. Might have been. I might have been you.

So your story keeps happening. There was this man in my country not long ago who got pie-eyed at his best friend's place. He climbed onto the roof of the house for a high dive into the swimming pool—drunk diving it's called—but he missed. A broken neck isn't always fatal these days, so he didn't quite make it to Hades. I don't think he should have sued his best friend, Elpenor. I didn't see you blaming Circe when that trap-door opened into Erebus.

There was a bit of the dog-in-the-manger about Odysseus, wasn't there, a bit of the know-it-all. He always wanted to be the one out front. He wanted to be the one lashed to the mast with the naked women serenading him while you and the others rowed by with beeswax in your ears. He didn't want anyone, and you least of all, beating him to the underworld. It must have been something to see his face when first shade to the blood offering was you. "You went faster by foot than I did with the black ship," he said, stiffly, to mask how peeved he was to be second. Black ship, black joke: that was your moment, Elpenor, still fresh after three thousand years.

&

I was a university student of pristine ignorance when I picked up Robert Kroetsch's *The Studhorseman*, the first book I ever read that seemed written for me. I loved those strange scenes set in the city I was living in—especially the winter carnival chaos of five hundred horses sprung from the Edmonton stockyards into a city centre paralyzed by blizzard. Those horses, giddyup with freedom, clopped in & out of my own haunts all night: the Palace of Sweets, the King Edward Hotel, the Rialto Theatre. I liked those places better with horses than without, & I'm no horse-fancier. Haven't been ever since Grade Six. Edmonton was for the first time fraught with metamorphosis. The city has never been the same since, &, now that I come to think of it, neither has anything else. & of course—not that I noticed back then—*The Studhorseman* is a wonky version of *The Odyssey*.

V

Agnes Walsh and Halldór Laxness

Much might be said about why my family and I were drawn to St. John's when we could have moved anywhere in Canada, but I'll settle for pointing to Agnes Walsh, her person and her poetry, neither of which I knew before sojourning here in 1997. Now that summer icebergs drifting by St. John's are visible from the upper floors of our Bond St. house, there's new life in an old metaphor: the Walsh in what follows is a mere tip of the berg of her book of poems, *In the Old Country of My Heart*, itself the tip of a vast berg of Newfoundland orature and literature strong enough, and ignored enough, that an old underdogger like me was bound to be drawn to it—drawn in through Agnes's poem, "Percy Janes Boarding the Bus," about speaking a revered name—*Percy Janes*—to hold a St. John's bus while the owner of the name hustles up. But Percy Janes is nobody to the bus driver. He waits out of politeness, not recognition:

> As the bus rumbled on
> I continued under my breath:
> "Ladies and gentlemen, Mr. Percy Janes,
> Newfoundland writer, poet,
> just boarded the number something-or-other."

> If this was Portugal,

a plaque would be placed
over the seat where he sat.

As it is, you have me
mumbling in the street
like a tourist in my own country.

Now, less of a tourist here than I was, I understand that "my country" is Newfoundland, not Canada, and that Percy Janes's *House of Hate* was *the* novel that moved Newfoundland writing into the twentieth century. I now see Agnes Walsh's poem as a backhanded manifesto. She wants the defining writers of her country known and valued by its citizens, like José Saramago in Portugal or Halldór Laxness in Iceland.

—◄o►—

I met my first Icelander in Alberta, on the orthopedic ward of the University Hospital in Edmonton while I was a relief orderly in the summer of 1963. He had badly hurt his back and had to spend the days stretched out on a Stryker frame. A big man for that narrow, rigid rig. Did he have to sleep on it? He was not allowed to turn on his own, so at regular intervals the nurse and I would make an Icelander sandwich by lowering the top (or bottom) of the frame onto him, securing it, strapping him in and then—Ready? On three. One, two, THREE—We'd spin him 180 degrees to his stomach (or back), then remove the bottom (or top) and there he'd be, still flat but with gravity pulling at a different side of him. I admired Mr. Stryker's invention and I greatly enjoyed flipping the Icelander.

I'm telling this to Agnes and Marnie in the kitchen of the

Fitzpatrick St. house in St. John's. How has it come up? I can't recall it ever coming up between 1963 and now, 1997. Something in the conversation released the Icelander and my conversation with him about Halldór Laxness's *Independent People,* my only contact with anything Icelandic up to 1963. Yes, he certainly had read the novel and he was mildly surprised that I had.

He might have been more surprised had he known how I came to the book. Laxness was not unknown in 1963. He had won the Nobel Prize in 1955, after all, "a remarkable and exceptional achievement," according to his translator, "for an author writing in a minority language in the smallest, youngest nation in the western world." This is forgetting the ancient sagas that Laxness folds into his novels, but what did I know of such things in high school? I happened on Iceland's most famous novel in the Oyen High School library, a random collection without any sense to it and the town's only library when I was a student in the late 1950s. There was a bigger library in my office when I retired from teaching. I read all the fiction in the high school library—everything except *The Golden Dog*. Out of all those shabby hardcovers, only *Independent People* stayed with me, that and *Les Misérables* in the fancy Valjean edition. Years later, when I bought the whole edition in a used bookstore, what was I looking for? The years before order, when I moved from book to book like water seeking its own level?

The hard, hard life of Bjartur of Summerhouses in *Independent People*, bleaker even than the lives of the Andrews and Vincent families in Bernice Morgan's Newfoundland novels—whatever Agnes said to recall this epic struggle of a nobody is lost in the story of her own fascination with Halldór Laxness that she told us at the kitchen table. I had the feeling that the story was surprised out of her. I could tell she was inside her life, not outside watching for anecdotes to dine out on. "We neither of us perform for strangers," says Miss Elizabeth Bennett to Mr. Darcy in *Pride and Prejudice*. Talk and not silence greases the gears of the world, but I don't talk, not freely, and I'm drawn to other stoneboats of speech: heavy, hard to get moving.

In Alberta, for me, Iceland was frozen in its name. Now, in Newfoundland, the name begins to melt as I discover that the whole country is heated by thermal springs, though a cup of coffee in Reykjavík costs five bucks Canadian—no wonder Icelanders charter planes to shop in Halifax and St. John's at stores displaying those *Velkomnir íslandsku gestir* signs—and that they won their fish wars while we lost ours.

Loving Halldór Laxness's writing, especially *The Atom Station*, Agnes decided one day in 1989 to call Mr. Laxness up. Newfoundland to Iceland, long distance, yes, but a thinkable distance, not like Alberta to Iceland in the late 1950s, though Iceland was then in one way more real to me than my own province: I'd never read about Alberta in a book.

How to reach Mr. Laxness without a number? Call information. Let's see, 011, 354, and then 0 for the Reykjavík operator.

I'm trying to reach Mr. Halldór Laxness, please.

Ah, Mr. Laxness. Mr. Laxness has three numbers. There is his house, his office, and his country house. That is where Mr. Laxness is at the moment, at his country house. But I regret to say that this is not an opportune time to call. At the moment Mr. Laxness is not well.

Is it serious?

No, an indisposition. But he is not taking calls.

Well then, thank you very much.

The life that sings, the rich green slope of the irony in Halldór Laxness's books, sprouted a need in Agnes to find out how the man was, but not to make herself known to him. She never spoke to him, not that day nor any other. It wasn't necessary. She had a satisfying semi-annual Laxness conversation with various Reykjavík operators for most of a decade, though it had been a few years since the last call when we talked in the Fitzpatrick St. house in 1997, the year before Halldór Laxness died.

―◄o►―

Hi Stan,

I'm taking your piece and I'm playing around with it. Not because there's anything wrong with it but because it got me interested in thinking back over it all again. Here goes a bit of fun. It's just my own fun. It does not mean that I think you should change a thing. I dial the info operator number and a woman answers in what I assume is Icelandic but it sounds a bit like English too. I say I am looking for a phone number for a Mr. Halldór Laxness, a writer from there who probably lives in Reykjavík or has an office number at the university. She cuts me off with yes, yes, of course Mr. Laxness, but he isn't at the university any longer. He has retired, he is an old man. Oh, I say, surprised at the stream of information, is he well known then in Iceland, I ask. Well, yes, of course, everyone knows him here, she tells me. I see, I say. I didn't know at the time that everyone in Iceland reads everything. Perhaps I'll take his home phone number then, I say. All right, hold a moment, I have it right here . . . ah, but that's right, she says, he isn't home now, he's in Bangkok at a world peace conference. But I'll give you his number and you can try him next week. I took it knowing I would never call. Six months later I dial the Icelandic info operator again and ask for his phone number, although I haven't lost it. The operator gives it to me. I ask if he is in

the country. Yes, she says, she thinks so. I ask how old Mr. Laxness is, if she knows. She pauses, says, let me see, one moment. I hear her speak in Icelandic. I hear several voices with questioning intonations. She comes back and says, we think eighty-five. Ah, I say, and do you know if his health is ok? Oh yes, she assures me, he is very active, travels a lot. Good I say. I tell her I am calling from Newfoundland and that he is a favourite writer of mine. I ask if she likes his work. Oh yes, he is an important writer for the Icelandic people. Yes, I say and I thank her. I called back about twice a year for some years to check on him. I used to imagine the operators would check in on him after their shift. Probably discuss something in one of his novels, but that was taking it too far. When I read a few years ago that he had passed away I couldn't help but think about the operators.
Love, Ag
(The real story)

―◦―

I was educated in the pseudo-science of close reading, Practical Criticism, to behave as though a text were a closed, autonomous signifying system. Put 'er in a bell jar and suck out all the air. (I saw that done in the Oyen high school lab.) Everlasting flowers are better than real ones. How could it be an ivory tower when you don't see any ivory?

The unfairness escalates. Shame on me for enjoying it.

But there's still something to be said for banishing most of the contextual whirlwind, if it's eventually allowed to blow back in, preferably a zephyr at a time. I asked Agnes to write something about the genesis of "When I Married Halldór Laxness," for example (see below), but not before I'd given the poem a loosened form of close reading—depending on my own resources to reach through technique towards the heart. I wanted to find out what I could say about it, more than any other poem in Agnes's book, because it seemed so impervious to criticism. I was actually trying to keep the author at arm's length, perhaps perversely feeling obliged to make it on my own but also convinced that she wouldn't, couldn't, have my sort of relationship with her poem, that no more than I was she an authority on her own work. I know from experience the gap that opens between writer and writing when the latter estranges itself. "When I Married Halldór Laxness," strange and dreamlike, seems clearly to have emerged from just such a letting go.

But a shade of the Agnes Walsh I know was always near while I read and considered and wrote about her work. I had both to keep my independence from this wraith and write nothing that would dismay it. Like poetry, criticism has nothing to do with placation or flattery. It has nothing to do with ingratiation, with ego, neither hers nor mine. But an intense respect, a deep courtesy towards the writer at full stretch might stretch me taut in my turn. That benign presence at my elbow reminds me that her work and mine are phases of the same enterprise. Real people meet in flesh-and-blood writing. The creative and the critical, compatible and autonomous:

> Reader, in your hand you hold
> A silver case, a box of gold.
> I have no door, however small,
> Unless you pierce my tender wall,
> And there's no skill in healing then
> Shall ever make me whole again.
> Show pity, Reader, for my plight:
> Let be, or else consume me quite.

The answer/title of this Jay Macpherson riddle/poem is "Egg," but the address to a Reader elevated into proper noun makes Egg a metaphor for Book.

I write about dead authors just as tenderly as about those living—tenderly and toughly—tough it is to think in and then out, in my humanly limited way, into the heart of the work and on out through layer upon layer of meaning towards . . . I wish I could drop that ellipsis. Untroubled participation in some continuum would sure be welcome. It's a strange occupation, this heartfelt service of what I can neither name nor know.

—◁o▷—

Two subjects I have always been interested in are humour and eroticism. Two others are places (and especially islands), and what makes up the culture of places. When I was a young girl I had a stamp collection with stamps only from islands. Big land mass has never interested me: Canada, Australia, China, Russia. But the little dots have: the Faroes, Iceland, Tobago, Newfoundland, Ireland, etc.

I wrote "When I Married Halldór Laxness" in the late 70s, not long after my father passed away. I was living at home then, having returned to be near my father in his old age. I had spent the ten years before that kicking around the U.S. and when I returned home I was struck by how much attention I was paying to detail, to small things in life, and to time passing. I spent a lot of time reading, a lot of time walking, thinking, imagining.

The atmosphere of the poem, the atmosphere I was living that is, was one of interest in light, wind, landscape, and observing. I believe that such a length of time in this "mind-frame" leaves one with pores more open and the mind "relaxed into a care-free sinking," if I can quote myself from another poem.

    While I was living this "atmospheric life" I was also going into St. John's twice a month by out-of-town taxi to take books from the MUN library back out home with me. I read them the way I had collected stamps. Islands. I carted back out in Dominion bags books from islands. Halldór Laxness was one of them. Aksel Sandemose was another (he is mentioned in the poem). Sandemose was from Denmark with a Norwegian mother, or perhaps it was the other way around. Sandemose had been in Newfoundland in the early part of the 20th century and wrote about his time here. So I stumbled upon his work also and read his truly amazing novel, The Werewolf. Then another, Horns for our Adornment. I remember the thrill I felt when I read in this novel: "The Fulton [a ship], was towed into St. John's, it being impossible to force the narrow channel without a fair wind." And later in the novel: "In Spain the climate was mild and people different. Here they were like they were in Norway. A disagreeable, everyday feeling of being at home. They spoke another language, but that was the only difference." It thrilled me beyond words to read this in a novel. Growing up we never read about ourselves or our landscape in fiction. And that a writer I admired had been here, in fact was harboured here, supposedly in Fogo after he killed a ship-mate who was cruel to him. The film Misery Harbour is Aksel Sandemose's novel and a loose version of his life.

    So there I was reading Laxness and Sandemose at the same time, two great novelists. Laxness' novel The Atom Station is about a young girl from the north of Iceland working as a house-maid in the city. The American military are at Keflavik wanting to set up an atomic tracking station. When I was growing up in Placentia, the American base in Argentia had flights, sailors going to Keflavik on an almost daily basis. All that seemed dream-like. I saw and heard *the planes leave Argentia every day for Keflavik. I had no idea what the Americans were doing there but the sailors talked of it a lot. I only saw the streaks the planes left in the clear blue sky.*

When I wrote the poem I was after reading these books by Laxness: World Light, The Happy Warriors, Christianity at Glacier, Salka Valka, *and* The Atom Station *(the latter several times). I was also asking my parents a lot of questions about their past and events that happened before I was born. I had also met with my cousin Sam B., to whom the poem is dedicated. Sam is 20–25 years my senior, a bit of a traveler, and a social misfit. We hit it off and traded books. He courted me which pissed my mother off. She thought he was too old and a cousin to boot. I liked being courted by him because he could old-fashion waltz, was saucy yet respectful, and he had a wonderful musky smell. So you get my drift. I was reading Laxness, I was drawn to Sam. I was living the atmospheric life of Nordic fiction, forbidden passion, and old Newfoundland, all mixed together with writing.*

For me it is an erotic poem. A literary, folkloric, dream-state fantasy of living on the edge of the earth.

—◄o►—

When I Married Halldór Laxness
(for Sam B.)

I watched the froth go down and the yellow liquid rise to meet it. I twisted the glass around and it tipped over and spilled on his arthritic knee. I looked to the side and didn't apologize. His beautiful bony fingers flicked off the foam in separate particles as if it was incidental lint he had finally noticed.

The decision is yours now.

He rubbed the liquid into his pant leg. I sighed. Either decision I make will kill something.

And so, you want to hang in this ether land forever?

Yes.

And if I pulled your hair?
And if I scalded your mouth?
And if I made a teepee of birch billets with you in the centre?

Look at me.

No.
He went away.

Next night the phone rang.
I'll meet you at Glacier and First Point. You must be exact.
I'll be there for three evenings.

For three nights I wore myself ragged but couldn't find where.
Friday evening the doorbell rang. He handed me two books by Aksel Sandemose. I put my fingers exactly where his warm fingerprints still lingered on the top book and closed the door. I read and waited.

(There was a tidal wave and a woman went from window to window with a candle in her hand as her house floated out the bay.

They rescued her in St. Lawrence.)

When you are ready, if ever, light your own candle.

Two years later, my hand shook as I held the match. His hair had greyed around the temples and he crippled shyly.

Five years later, two babies look hauntingly like him. He is chopping wood in the backyard. He stops.

Look at me. I fooled you years ago. Glacier is in Iceland and I tore out all the pages where it was written in that book. Do you regret that we called the babies Abstract and Zero? Come feel Aunt Hilda and Didymus under my fingernails.

His gentle laugh ripped the night sky, and I got pregnant again.

◄o►

What does all this mean? I always hear that question voiced by the bewildered witness to a metaphysical gunfight in Ed Dorn's *Slinger*. The gun "occurs" in the Slinger's hand and with it he "describes" his opponent:

> What does the foregoing mean?
> I asked. Mean?
> my gunslinger laughed
> Mean?
> Questioner, you got some strange

obsessions, you want to know
what something *means* after you've
seen it, after you've *been* there
or were you *out* during
That time?

The gunslinger is nothing if not hip. He's a hip, intellectual cowboy demi-god, so he isn't going to be down on interpretation. I think the person who wrote him is saddling "I" with the common paralysis of a mind stormed with experience not immediately intelligible. Jesus, Slinger might say, is that all you can think to ask? That is the *first* thing you want to know? You can't just *go* with it for a spell? You want a fucking paraphrase?

Well, it doesn't really do to sneer at the uncomprehending, seeing that it's you and me. And we do want to know. We'd rather understand than be hip. We might begin by improving the question. What's *going on* in the above? Let's ask that. It frees us right away to think about genre and technique.

First, a catalogue of the obvious—which immediately changes the genre, from poem into story. "When I Married Halldór Laxness" looks like a poem (and Agnes thinks of it as such; prose poem—no line breaks) because the narrative is so stark, but the piece has narration and dialogue and the bones of a plot. At the centre of the plot (so reduced as to be almost all centre) is a January–May pair of characters, first attracted but at odds, who move closer to each other in the course of the story. The time scheme is linear. It spans seven years of the relationship. After the first scene we jump into the next night, then to the next week, then two years later, five years later. The final scene is the first one given in the present tense; that shift in tense reveals a present from which the rest of the (past tense) tale is retrospectively told.

The most dreamlike, least developed aspect of narrative technique is setting. When the woman spills beer on the pant leg of a man, she presumably does it in a room. The room is in her house, presumably, since he's the one who leaves. The phone, the doorbell, the door: these bare details also imply a house. Seven years later, a house (the same one?) is implied by its back yard. And that's it. "Glacier is in Iceland" gives no clue as to where the house might be, since the woman has been fooled into thinking she can reach it from where she lives, which may be but is not identifiable as Newfoundland. Glacier is not in Iceland, not on the map anyway, though glaciers are; rather, it's a fictional place in Laxness's allegorical novel, *Christianity in Glacier*. Nor is the parenthesis (containing a scene from the aftermath of the 1929 Newfoundland tidal wave) locational, since the woman in the dislodged floating house has no obvious connection with the two characters. This two-sentence parenthetical unit has as much setting as the rest of the piece, however: a house, a bay, a town—St. Lawrence near the tip of the Burin Peninsula.

The narrator is a young(ish?) woman involved in a strange, arbitrary relationship with an older man, perhaps even an aged man who yet has the potency to father children, though in a manner comic and more of myth than biology (the third pregnancy is caused by a laugh). The story opens at a moment of crisis, of decision. Tension between the two characters is established by a bit of aggressive play with a glass of beer. He has most of the speech. She sighs but otherwise speaks only two words, "Yes" and "No." Reticence aside, she is not passive. She is unapologetic about spilling beer on him; she decides immediately to "hang in this ether land," though she knows the decision will cost her; she refuses to look at him when he commands her to. (He seems to be raising obstacles, testing her. Will your decision stand if you know in advance that I'll mistreat you, and unpredictably?) Yet she is obsessed with him. She attempts to find the impossible rendezvous he appoints; she has a lover's reaction to the gift of Aksel Sandemose books, matching her fingers to his prints. None of the riddling deters her; she doesn't give up on him.

The turning point, the moment of mutual commitment, seems to come in the section beginning "two years later." Two sentences carry the bones of a (marriage?) ceremony, perhaps involving a candle. There is a match in her trembling hand, and she may be lighting the candle that signals her readiness. (Only adjacency connects this candle with the one carried from window to window of the floating house.) Possibly she is now repeating the "Yes" she offered two years ago, though it would be stretching to identify readiness to "hang in this ether land" with readiness to marry. The adverb "shyly," though strange modifying "crippled" (a verb here, usually a noun) suggests a change in him, a mellowing.

Five years later, the two of them are (still?) together, if we can go by the babies and his back-yard chopping, signs of domestic arrangement. His conversation is as enigmatic as ever. Since he's clearly the guy for her, she must absolutely *love* non sequitur. He still demands her attention, her gaze at least, and he reminds her (as the story flashes back) of a command that he now reveals to have been a joke: he lured her to a rendezvous that he made sure she couldn't locate. Were those torn-out pages from a guide book or a novel? Is that "ether land" fiction? If I didn't know Agnes to be a devoted reader of Halldór Laxness, would it occur to me to wonder if the marriage has to do with the relationship between fiction and a loving reader?

In a tale so curtailed, little becomes much. Climax and dénouement require a single sentence. "Gentle laugh," added to "shyly," suggests either that he has mellowed or that all his earlier threats were a front to discourage too easy involvement in an inappropriate and bumpy relationship. A few facts can be established about the story, then, but I've had to be tentative and ask a lot of questions. There are further questions: Abstract and Zero? These are unlikely names for babies either in real life (with apologies to Zero Mostel) or in any fiction with pretensions to realism. The names do frame the whole gamut of alphabet, A to Z, and they might tease certain minds towards philosophy and mathematics. Didymus? The Greek name ("twin") of St. Thomas, the doubter who needed and received physical evidence of Christ's resurrection. "Under my fingernails?" Some things will have to be left hanging in the ether. But then I don't expect the piece to mean piecemeal. The whole thing is dreamlike, riddling, nonsensical. It teeters on an edge between the ominous and the humorous. In it there is this sense of a woman prepared to sacrifice something in order to remain in a (metaphorical) land presided over by an unintelligible but compelling man with the almost god-like power of creating life by laughing.

◄o►

If the foregoing has any use it's to show that conventional literary analysis will get us somewhere with "When I Married Halldór Laxness." The terms that work best were shaped to discuss fiction, which means either that what I first took to be a poem should be reclassified as a story or that, at a certain degree of truncation, story becomes poem.

All that's clearly missing from what I've said so far is everything—the spirit of the piece. Or am I nearing it with my hunch that the dreamlike story is a transmutation of Agnes's relationship with Laxness's books? That impregnating laugh, for instance: mythic, yes, and with the feel of heroic, Laxnessian hyperbole. From *The Atom Station*: "And Geiri of Midhouses laughed—that laugh that would suffice to build a cathedral, even on the summit of Mount Hekla."

One of Mario's Ruoppolo's questions for Pablo Neruda is left unanswered in the film *Il Postino*: "The whole world is a metaphor for something else?" Neruda takes the question seriously, but he wants to sleep on it and it's easy to see why. Life in the film moves on and the question never comes up again. I wonder if a similar question should be asked of "When I Married Halldór Laxness," since it's both compelling and enigmatic from one end to the other: is the poem a metaphor for something else in its entirety? I think there's a roundabout way of answering by way of material that might even have been presented first except that it fell beyond the reach of unaided interpretation. Only when my own thinking and researching has been exhausted would I consider asking the writer anything about her text. I don't want any approach foreclosed by deference to the writer. A critic in the pocket of a writer is a puppet or a parrot, though a critic with nothing to offer the writer should find another line of work. But it would be silly to ignore unsolicited aid, background information provoked merely by praising "When I Married Halldór Laxness" to Agnes Walsh. What came out had nothing to do with Laxness; it was about the courtship of the Sam B. to whom she dedicated the poem.

So the mild eroticism of "When I Married Halldór Laxness" owes as much to the person of Sam Bambrick as to anything in Laxness's books. Maybe the birch billets do too, not being Icelandic. "Chunks of firewood in Newfoundland are junks, unless they happen to be *birch* junks, when they become billets" (Harold Horwood, quoted in *Dictionary of Newfoundland English*). Before the piece could be written, there had to be another marriage or merging of two affections: Sam Bambrick and Halldór Laxness. Whatever Laxness and his books contributed to the writing, Sam lent his attention, his body past its prime, and perhaps a single Newfoundland word. Knowing this only confirms something unsurprising: the poem is an invention.

A further conversation with Agnes, this time about Laxness's *The Atom Station* (which I read on her recommendation) produced another stray piece of information: First Point is in Placentia. I intended to exhaust Laxness's novels searching for First Point and was both relieved and disappointed when the location was handed to me. Never mind. Knowing it and knowing what to do with it are two different things. The first thing that comes to mind (besides more Newfoundland content) is the outrage to logic in the challenge to coordinate an actual place in one country with a fictional place in another. The poem/story is built on such wonderful outrages, so that's nothing new. What is new is the thought, if we step away from the literal, that readers do leap effortlessly from life to fiction, and do it all the time. Fixed in this country, we tour that one; from any actual place we travel widely in the realms of gold. Placentia, Newfoundland, meets Glacier, Iceland, as Agnes Walsh meets Halldór Laxness (and Laxness meets Sam Bambrick), and they all mingle agreeably in a reader. I may have been on to something with my thought that the piece is indirectly about reading, homage to fiction so potent as to invade one's very life. What could be a more potent salute to life-changing writing than a piece of writing-in-return that dissolves the boundary between life and literature, superimposing one on the other? I'm still asking, but I've thought my way around to a good question: is the meaning of the piece this delighted and delightful doubling, life and literature impossibly and decisively occupying the same dream?

&

none of Agnes Walsh's writing—not even the intimate lyric poetry of *In the Old Country of My Heart*—is mere self-expression. It's all about restoring to the culture of the Cape Shore, her own rich & distinctive region of Newfoundland, the dignity it deserves. It has been too easy, even for natives, to dismiss Newfoundland as some sort of quaint edge of nowhere. (I don't think that E. Annie Proulx reinforces that impression in *The Shipping News*, but a lot of Newfoundlanders do.) So it's ironic that, when Agnes & I finished the presentation that became "Agnes Walsh & Halldor Laxness," the call for questions immediately produced a typical rumination about the love-hate ambivalence felt by many Newfoundlanders for their place. To lift the heart, there's the intricate elemental landwash & layers of distinctive culture; to make it plummet there's the have-not economy, with notorious giveaways by Newfoundlanders themselves, & heartrending outmigration. Fierce pride & low self-esteem. A compact, cynical variation on this bind appears in William Rowe's novel, *Clapp's Rock*, when Percy Clapp, a Joey Smallwood figure, speaks of

> that bizarre form of pride of place possessed in embryo by all poor and isolated peoples (don't ask me why—it defies reason—I only use the materials at hand), the belief that they are in some paradoxical way better than all the other peoples and countries to which they feel inferior.

Somewhere behind such ruminations is almost always the humiliating 1933 resignation of Newfoundland's responsible government by a country honourably bankrupt but badly run, followed by over a decade of colonial rule & then, in 1948, confirmation of subordinate status by absorption into another nation. Only to become a national joke. Many

Newfoundlanders, Agnes Walsh among them, have understandably never become Canadians, not in spirit. There is a Newfoundland nation, but nobody can have it.

Not much a CFA (Come From Away) can say about such affliction other than to commiserate. & watch for signs of healing humour. There is a Newfoundland branch of subversive minority humour, & one fork of the branch is a sophisticated & eloquent self-disparagement, a far cry from the patronizing Newfie joke that outsiders attempt at their peril. After the formal session, the ruminator told a joke on Newfoundlanders that I have too much sense to repeat, even if I could remember it.

W

Twelve Bars

for Stuart Pierson 1934–2001

The Duke of Duckworth

Got the blues, but I'm too damn mean to cry

Being here right now with my feet in these socks, in these very shoes resting on that blue patch of rug, the rug laid down on that new birch floor—it's very strange. Wearing *these* clothes today rather than any of the others hanging in my closet or folded in my drawers. Sitting on this couch and glancing into exactly that and no other blue sky where it meets the deeper blue ocean just at that grey band of cloud I won't ever see again. A jet trailing jet stream far above. Strange that for this one instant in all the millions of unregarded moments passing I should *know* I'm here, now, with the sun bright on the green, the maroon, the grey, the rust, and the blue, all the clapboard houses stepped down Victoria towards Gower. That I should be seeing it all and hearing the hammers pounding on that renovating house on the corner down there over the grand hum of the city. Lucky to be here now, period.

    Woke up from a week of the blues, when I couldn't get away from myself at all. Only so far as keeping an eye on the dog after she shat all over three floors of the house. One bad week alone with my miserable lonesome and that goddamn dog with her guilty eyes.

The Yellow Dory

Nobody knows you when you're down and out

Welcome to St. John's, says Fergus O'Byrne from the stage. Simon told him at the break we're here from Ontario and now he's addressing our table. Thanks for coming out. We appreciate it. Just don't take any of our jobs. This gets a laugh. Fergus O'Byrne and Dermot O'Reilly, two-thirds of the legendary folk group Ryan's Fancy. At the end of the evening we approach the stage with thanks, and I don't know any better than to make a joke. We promise not to take any of your jobs, I say, but we did pick a few of your blueberries. I thought that would be a tiny bit funny—it wasn't the moon of humour I was shooting at—but Fergus O'Byrne hasn't a clue what I'm talking about. He just stares at me though those round, wire-rimmed glasses that looked funky all night but now seem vaguely teutonic. I'd like to blame the silence on him since I'm only returning a remark he made himself not thirty minutes ago. But I blame my miserable self. Middle-aged and ain't got no sense yet hardly. If I had a dollar for every strained silence I've created in my lifetime, I'd be rich. Have mercy, I'd be a rich man today.

The Peter Easton

> *When I get you in my sights*
> *Boom, Boom, out goes the lights*

Ron Hynes wrote "No Change" with Murray MacLauchlan to say how hard it is living in a too-small town with no prospects. In the song, St. John's is emptied right out. Everybody gone somewhere else, looking for work.

> You could fire off a cannon
> At the top of Long's Hill
> And a Gulliver's Taxi
> Might be all that you'd kill

But the streets were not completely empty that time I was out for a run in December '97, finally on the flat after the climb up Long's Hill, just past Ches's Fish and Chips, when a hard-packed snowball smacked into the side of my head. And whoever it was had led me so perfectly was gone. Vanished. No witnesses. You could fire off a cannon. Shit!

But I shook it off—what the hell, it's only winter sports—and started up Pennywell. And pretty soon I started to feel better than I had before I got hit. That was an excellent throw, after all: small moving target, follow-through cut short on account of having to duck out of sight. There must be some kind of lesson here. There must be something we can learn. Yes there is, and here it comes: when you take a mean shot to the head and yet admire the asshole who did it, you've got to be some kind of a loser.

The Fat Cat

You better come on in my kitchen

To hear the legendary Roger Howse. Stuart says no one plays the blues any better. We think Stuart knows. He and Janet first heard Roger Howse at The Bear and Bull just after they got married, when they were poor as church mice. They didn't mean to go in there at all, with only a buck seventy-five to their names, but somebody hauled them in and somehow they drank until closing time on just that buck seventy-five. There was a moose head hanging on the wall, Janet says, with a red light in one eye and a green light in the other. This was about twenty years ago. We're hearing about it in the kitchen of 70 Prescott, once owned by Johnny Burke, "the bard of Prescott Street." Outside of which may demons mass and hiss and gnash their terrible teeth till the cows come home, because we're inside, warm, King's X. Stuart says he liked it best when Roger took a guitar solo. His eyes would roll up under his closed lids and you could tell he was gone, man, gone. Those were the days. Stuart doesn't say so, but we can tell.

There's a man with a beer gut setting up. He's chain-smoking, impatient, fussing with the equipment. Who's that guy, I ask. That's Roger Howse, Stuart says, that's my man. Roger Howse may be terrific but he sure can't be famous. He's both headliner and roadie. As far as he's concerned, the first set stinks. He isn't hearing what he wants. He's pissed off. He keeps fiddling with the amp. He sure can play the blues, and sing it too—Stuart was right—but let him leave that amp alone, let him go inside himself. I like the look of that Sean Harris. I recognize him from El Viento Flamenco. Roger Howse likes his looks too. Sean Harris brings in a new amp for the second set and the new amp works perfectly. Roger Howse beams and Sean Harris beams, and set two is all the blues. Jesus, set two is the blues itself. The first time Roger's eyes roll up under his lids we turn around to smile at Stuart and his eyes are full of tears. Ah, Stuart. *These* are the days too. They have to be. We didn't know you, we didn't know you and Janet back then.

The Rose and Thistle

There's a dead cat on the line

The air in this bar is blue. You're a smoker by default. The performers can't wait for the break. They'll all sit down at the table nearest the window and light up. If someone turned the lights on you'd see the smoke hanging thick as a fog rolled in through The Narrows. Your clothes are soaking it up. They already smell of your time alone here, listening to this English Department reggae and waiting for Ben to join you when he's caught up. Just to sit and quietly talk a little for a damn change. Pour a little something on your melancholy. Hope it doesn't get out of control. You don't want to be climbing Prescott with red eyes again. You can explain smoke but not tears. Ah, but this town is too small. This town you love is too fucking small, or else Jack and Bev would not be walking in right now and paying their four bucks and coming over to join you. Which means that Ben will not. His sick smile behind the bar is telling you that. And here you go. Here goes another night of jolly pretend. And it's not angels hovering up Prescott and past Rawlins Cross, it's not angels waiting on Monkstown Road. It's not. Nobody's going to be flying away tonight. There's a brand-new kitchen to hear all about. That's what there is, that's all there is for you tonight. Better face up to that and pay attention. Better squash your little middle-class grief and fucking get on with it.

The Blarney Stone

> *I don't care what Mr Crump don't allow*
> *I'm gonna barrelhouse anyhow*

When Folk Club was at The Blarney Stone we sometimes walked down without knowing who was on. Open mic is often the best part anyhow. That's how we found Terri-Lynn Eddy in full cry. "Santa Claus Blues." Was it December? Who cares. Give me that big, raw voice wrapped around "Santa Claus Blues" any time of year. It was the first and last time I saw every single patron in The Blarney Stone shut up and listen. Even the musicians at Folk Club are talkers, you see, so most of the time you could drop an anvil in there and nobody'd notice. It's a mystery to me why performers don't slit their wrists after some of these gigs. But on this night nobody was even playing the VLTs. She's only fifteen, I heard somebody say. Is that possible? A fifteen-year-old Mama from Around the Bay holding everybody in this bar in the palm of her hand. Half a dozen girlfriends were with her, crowded around a table a few feet from the stage, which is just a low riser in front of a bay window. The friends came into their own when Terri-Lynn ran out of encores. That's something else I never saw at Folk Club, not before or since—an encore. "She Taught Me How to Yodel," one yelled. I'm not going to yodel, spat Terri-Lynn, and there was the kid behind the woman belting out that raunch. How did she get a bye into the blues? I sure hope it wasn't coming out of her life. Well, she was no Wilf Carter, but she could yodel. As the song began, one of the friends suddenly flicked on a lighter and started to wave it back and forth like at the big concerts and another friend quickly suppressed her. "Santa Claus Blues" one more time, then the door-prize draw, the break, and a set of traditional jigs and reels and polkas with button accordion, fiddle, bohdran, and guitar.

Now it's two years later, and Terri-Lynn has been discovered. There are posters for the Terri-Lynn Eddy Band all over town. Close-up on her face with sultry eyes looking out over dark glasses. Well, she wasn't going to stay fifteen, and it's none of my damn business anyway. I just hope she's still wailing for the love of it.

Johnny Burke's

> *Don't drink a black cow's milk*
> *Don't you eat a black hen's egg*

In "Nonlecture One," e.e. cummings makes his audience "a strictly egocentric proposition." He means to speak about himself, as Harvard University asked him to, but first he pauses, having led his listeners perfectly, and then he hits them with this: "who, if I may be so inconsiderate as to ask, isn't egocentric? Half a century of time and several continents of space, in addition to a healthily developed curiosity, haven't yet enabled me to locate a single peripherally situated ego." Surprised laughter. You can hear laughter on the tape, but not the tears of sorrow and pleasure mixed, as cummings lovingly tells of his courageous mother's car accident—all that glass in her head and still thinking of others first—the collision that killed his father, "than whom no father on earth ever loved or ever will love his son more profoundly."

But I digress. That's the way I am. Rather than look at you and talk to you I jump away into the words of others, those distances I love. It keeps me standing still in the very socks and shoes I told you about. For all the good it did either of us. Stock-still in this particular miserable cypher, this circumference of a dot.

Green Sleeves

Black snake hangin round my door

Ugh, there's a nasty leech. I'm not sitting out here! It's a leech, all right. Look there. They suck your blood.

They do?

Damn right they do. I'm not sitting out here ever again!

(Patron misidentifies slug)

Finnigan's Wake I

Bring me a pillow for my poor head
A hammer to knock out my brains

He has already broken off in the middle of a song, left the room, returned, started up—impressive—precisely where he quit. Our table is a few feet from the mic, so when he starts to cough and choke again he can easily step out, grab my pint, and take a couple of gulps. Without a by-your-leave. Well, it may be my beer, but his need is greater. Throat trouble is the least of what he's up against. The whole Liberal caucus is in the room behind him. They've had a pleasant Liberal dinner downstairs at NaGeira's and they've all come up here for after-dinner drinks and a smoke. There's no cover for restaurant customers—a good way to clear out lingering diners but a poor way to gather an audience. The caucus is raucous. Singer? What singer? The one who has been glancing behind him with blue murder in his eye. If he hadn't once met the gaze of Chuck Furey, Minister of Culture and Tourism, paying what attention he could, we might have had the spectacle of one of the world's best singer-songwriters losing it, running amok in a room full of elected philistines. But a spectacle is to watch, and we wouldn't have watched that. The unofficial Ron Hynes fan club would have risen as one and charged the other room.

But there is no rising. Even with another glug of my beer, Ron can't finish the set, breaks early.

We know his marriage is on the rocks, we know about the drugs. "My professional life is skyrocketing," he said to Kathleen Lippa of *The Express*; "my personal life's a mess. I'm a handful—a dangerous entity in the world. Have nothing to do with me." Big smile. But there's been no smiles tonight; his professional life is nosediving. So where's he going with his guitar? Where can he possibly go and what can he possibly do to recover after that?

Finnigan's Wake II

> *After all my hard travellin*
> *Things about comin my way*

"It's a profession full of pitfalls. And you need personal power to survive inside of it. And lots of it. On a daily basis. That's the only way to survive in this business. Nobody else can save you. You have to save yourself. Every day. *Every* day." That was in the interview too. Here's another version: after thirty years in the profession, his ego crushed so often it's past anthracite to diamond, Ron Hynes could cut glass. Of course he's coming back out to face the demons of indifference.

Mind you, it's not the same bar. The Liberal ranks are thinner. A big crowd of music lovers, Anita Best among them, has hustled over after the Ben Heppner concert. Anita's in charge of the Bards and Ballads Series and invited Ron for this gig. Has she heard about the first set disaster or is she merely reading this crowd? Maybe she just wants to hear "Tickle Cove Pond." Anyway, after his first song, a new one not yet a winner with the audience, Anita has a word with Ron. "Tickle Cove Pond" is exactly right. It even snags a couple of Liberals. They swing their chairs around and sing the chorus with the rest of us. Then "Old Brown's Daughter," then "Sonny's Dream." Now everyone is hooked. The bar fills with our voices:

> Still got my high school jacket
> Still got my high school ring
> Tucked in a corner of my wallet
> Is a tattered photo of The King
>   Yet I have to cry
>   Starin' back at silent eyes

> I saw a star burn out last night
> South of cryer's paradise

Barb—she plays violin with the St. John's Symphony Orchestra—leans over and speaks into my ear: Ben Heppner was great, but this is better. Ron's in the groove and we're in it with him, now belting out the chorus of that beautiful nonsense written for his daughter:

> Who's the bestest baby
> in the wholy whirly-perleedies?
> The wholy whirly-perl
> Wholy whirly-perl
> Wholy whirly-perleedies
> Whirly-perleedies

That woman by the bar—I must learn her name because her face always displays the wonderful lift I feel when Ron Hynes and his listeners meet exactly halfway. *These* are the days, *this* is where it's at, and we know it. The city has grown and grown tonight. Right now it's the one we'd choose—no question—the very one we'd choose over any other city in the whole
wide

whirly-perleedies.

Erin's Pub

> *Mp [pomt bptuj pf is s;pggomg tjrpigj tje fdrozz;e after c;psomg to,e. — dpwm*

What's *with* these sound systems? This one will not adjust to Jim Joyce's satisfaction. It's going to be another long night for the performer. Not a disaster this time (and no sudden rising of the corpse), just a kind of hot-lead-seeping-into-the-marrow sort of heaviness, I'd say. Though maybe it's just me, antennae quivering, picking this up and laying it down on Mr. Joyce—*James* Joyce on the posters and his CD. Stuart and Janet brought me down to hear him. He has already played "Kansas City" for Stuart—catcalls from the Irish patrons of this Irish bar—who starts for Kansas tomorrow. For research, not one of those "pretty little women." In the second set, Jim will play "Flower of Scotland," and Stuart's eyes will leak, his arms wave about in heartfelt parody of Scots national fervour. Stuart being of the Seattle Piersons.

James Joyce. The name makes me shiver, though of course this is not the mole-sighted literary giant. It's the Irish tenor of the same name, now dividing his time between Florida and Goose Bay. He's in demand in Florida bars, and he likes the golf down there, but his wife has been transferred to Labrador. How does he like Goose Bay? Well . . . the hiking is great.

Not an outright disaster. But yesterday was Flip Janes's funeral and the whole arts community is way down. I saw Jim's shoulders shaking during the service. And the sound muddy tonight. And the lead singer for Shanneyganock stepping onto the stage just like he owned it and fiddling with the sound board. Then weaseling his way into an invitation to do a couple of songs in that rich Stan Rogers baritone and the audience loving him. And me confessing that I break eighty once in a long while, while Jim's best so far is eighty-six. All of which probably amounts to nothing but me laying my weight on him. You can lift the world if that little interior gyroscope is whirling true, but I sense a wobbling. Maybe it takes one to know one.

One time, Janet says, it was late, and she and Stuart were about to leave the Joyces's house when Jim thought of a song. So he got out the guitar and, four hours later . . . Stuart is full of wonder: how can any one person store up all that music? Where does an Irish tenor reach inside himself to pull out "Kansas City" when he hasn't sung it in a decade? Stuart himself can remember but a half dozen songs, and one is "They're Moving Father's Grave To Build a Sewer."

Those wonderful tenor pipes and all that music—you want it lining the heart or the soul or the pit of the stomach, whatever it is the demons go for. If he has demons. If they aren't all mine. No point both of us slogging through the drizzle after last call, down Water to George Street, up George past all those Guinness-Book-of-Records bars—a bad mistake, when you're already down, to drift like a cypher past all that pulsing life—back to New Gower, Duckworth, up Prescott home. No point the both of us being solitary in the bosom of our families.

The Ship Inn

You never miss the water
Till your well run dry

You had your night music. Been and gone. The honey sweetened your tongues and there was nobody watching, least of all yourselves. Everything sweet and slick in the honey moon. You will never, never slide like that again. You want to seal it all up in amber, all you lost the second you lay down out there. Habit already creeping on you when you rose.

But won't the honey moon slide around next month?

Who told you that? Moon doesn't move. You turn around her. Go back outdoors. Don't say "velvet meniscus," don't give me "engorged with its population of the night." Just drop your tone way down and go back out. There's something bright and slick across the curve of that dark pool. Go back and lay your cheek down there. Lay yourself down and take a look.

It's not the same, is it? It's all changed. What did you expect?

I know only one up-side to Stuart's death in 2001. At least he was spared knowing that Michael Winter's *This All Happened*, the book that all but made him pack it in—not just the book, Janet said, *reading!*—won the inaugural Winterset Award for Newfoundland writing in any genre.

Sitting across from Stuart at his kitchen table I tried to tell him—his eyes actually bugging out in astonishment—what I loved about the book he hated: the humour, the crisp style, the meandering minimal plot, a quest for Lydia & love. He wasn't having it.

Impasse.

I wish I'd thought to tell him of a parallel stalemate reached by a literary couple, friends of mine since divorced. Both had submitted work to *Grain*—this was in the '70s—& received their replies in the same mail. He'd been rejected, so she couldn't very well exult in her acceptance; she'd been accepted, so he couldn't very well denounce the editor's vile literary judgment. There's your entirely unsatisfying balance of forces equal & opposite. There's your perfect piss-off.

Stuart swallowed his outrage; I swallowed my amusement, each of us sharing an edge of the other's emotion. Then we were back to loving each other across the gulf of difference irreducible.

X

The Sound Barrier

> there are knives in the air
> all around the poorly loved
> Robin Blaser

I

I keep returning to a core image of Himani Bannerji's "The Sound Barrier." Here is a restless eight-year-old girl with nothing to do on a hot afternoon. Her mother wants her to sleep but she can't sleep and she's bored. What to do? Well, there's a book lying on the bed next to her mother's hand. Not just any book, though the eight-year-old doesn't yet know its cultural significance. It's Kashi Das's version of *The Mahabharata*. She knows many of the stories in it by heart, but she has never tried to read it. I'll return to what happens when she begins after I've placed this young reader—poised on the brink of the fortunate fall into print—in the context of what leads up to it in "The Sound Barrier." That scene is brilliantly prepared for by the laying on and then peeling back of layers or circles of cultural complexity. The first section is a feminist Indian folktale; the two following sections interpret and enrich the tale by showing non-Bengali readers how little s/he could grasp of the cultural coding in that apparently transparent mythic narrative.

The first section, "In the First Circle," opens with an epigraph from *The Mahabharata*, the beginning of a story in which Maharaja

Yayati wishes to exchange his wealth and power for the youth of one of his sons. The passage is in English, but with alternate translations or clarifications in brackets. Are the annotations quoted from the source or supplied by Bannerji? (In the most recent publication of her text, Bannerji identifies herself as the translator, but I'm trying to hold first and subsequent readings together.) Annotations of an epigraph would seem unnecessarily fussy prefacing any sort of text except one that makes language and translation a central theme. Once this theme is identified, as it could be only on a second reading, then one can see why the narrative proper of "In The First Circle" is in English, but, again, presented as a translation, and with transliterated phrases of the original incorporated. "*Beside me, the little grassy glade that I stand in, is a forest—ghana, swapadashankula—dense and full of dangerous beasts of prey.*" The original is Bengali, but until that is spelled out in the text a Western reader can identify it only as one of the languages of India.

The story is a self-interpreting allegory in the dream-logic of folktale. When Bannerji quotes two passages from *The Mahabharata* of Kashi Das, the first, according to Amitava Roy, is in "*Sadhu Bhasa* i.e. Sanskritized Bengali," and the next is apparently Kashi Das remarking on *The Mahabharata* and his retelling, in "*Chalit Bhasa* i.e. colloquial 'vulgar . . .' Bengali spoken by all and sundry, not just the Elite's language." Bannerji has not tagged all the linguistic levels in her own narrative. It tells of a narrator's fraught journey into her mother's womb where she meets idols representing the three phases of Mother, "*as she was, as she has become, and as she will be,*" and ends, in a sudden temporal reversal, with the narrator being born. A bald summary omits the complexity and the dramatic intensity of the story. It has a passionate, self-reflexive, didactic edge uncharacteristic of folktales like those collected by the Brothers Grimm.

Kapalkundala, the wanderer's guide, has a feminist agenda: "*Woman's body is both the source of uncleanliness and life, she said. So have the sages spoken. Let us go into that gate, that body, she said, to ascertain the verity of their famed masculine, Brahmin intellect and pronouncements.*" Mother "as she has become," then, is "*a woman, crushed beneath the weight of a male figure, with one hand over her abdomen protecting the life within.*"

The story is drenched with fear, sadness, and loss, and the melancholy persists to the end, which is far too abrupt to be happy: "The violence of my own tears and anguish woke me and I heard a wail as I opened my eyes. I was born." It would be a mistake to think of this primal experience only in negative terms. Coming so close to Mother, living or writing through painful birth into painful life—the experience churns with emotion; it's charged with energy.

Having wound up to that birth-wail, Bannerji's text now abruptly relaxes into another kind of intensity. The second part, "Breaking the Circle: Writing and Reading a Fragment," begins:

> Reader, you have just finished reading a piece put together by me from fragments of language, memories, textual allusion, cultural signs and symbols. It is clearly an attempt to retrieve, represent and document something. But what sort of text is it? Does it speak to you? And what does it say?

This part of "The Sound Barrier" addresses other South Asian women:

> Are you also trying to capture alive, and instead finding yourself caught up in a massive translation project of experiences, languages, cultures, accents

and nuances? Are you also struggling with the realization that you are self-alienated in the very act of self-expression?

"I don't write for white middle-class readers," Bannerji says in an *Other Solitudes* interview with Arun Mukherjee, another Canadian from India, "I write for you and me." Which may seem to spell out her intention to respond to exclusion with exclusion, but probably just identifies the most intimate core of her audience. Only if someone like Bannerji appears in my own innermost eye could I expect to find myself in hers. Yes, the text is prickly for readers like me, but that swells my empathy. I assume that Bannerji and Mukherjee are not holing up, when they do so, just for the hell of it. Besides, "self-alienated in the very act of self expression" sounds familiar. "If we live in space which is radically in question for us," Dennis Lee says in "Cadence, Country, Silence: Writing in Colonial Space," "that makes our barest speaking problematic to itself. For voice does issue in part from civic space. And alienation in that space will enter and undercut our writing, make it recoil upon itself, become a problem to itself." If Lee and Bannerji had said nothing else about their experience with language, their relation to it might seem almost identical. But Lee is speaking of the potential to be alienated inside a language so second-nature that you have to surprise yourself into detecting falseness in it. For Bannerji, discourse difficulties are both multiple and palpable.

The next four pages of "Breaking the Circle" cover various levels of difficulty in writing. To the common struggle to communicate anything of importance, even in one's first language, is added the second-language barrier:

In another language, I am another person, my life another life. When I speak of my life in India, my mother or others there, I have a distinct feeling of splintering off from my own self, or the actual life that is lived, and producing an account, description, narrative—what have you—which distinctly smacks of anthropology and contributes at times to the paraphernalia of Orientalism.

Now, these pages are eloquent enough, but they are "about." They are telling not showing. Bannerji has emerged from the trance of her folktale into self-reflexive critical discourse (passing from passion to reason, story to argument), and now she shifts course again, not back into the mythic world but back into story, autobiographical realism this time, to tell of the childhood context that naturalized *The Mahabharata* in her domestic life. The epic may be exotic to the few Western readers aware of it, she says, but it's alive in her Bengali culture as the Norse sagas still live in Iceland. "Its presence in this text signifies not a detour into the classics, but an involuntary gesture to my mother's and my grandmother's world—in fact, to myself as a child. This is what it feels like from the inside." Then begins the scene I alluded to earlier and will quote soon: the small reader about to sound the print of *The Mahabharata*.

There follows a third section, "Breaking the Circle: Mother-Tongue," also autobiographical, which gives childhood and reading in both Bengali and English an even wider context, further decoding the initial folktale. The two languages, we find, are two different worlds. To the young Himani Bannerji, Bengali is pleasure while English is duty; Bengali is nationalist; English is international; Bengali is Mother, both her own mother and the three-phased goddess, and "the interior world of home"; English is the world of father and brothers, the "public world outside [which] held the serious business of earning money, achievement [and] success." The greatest particular revelation for me in this section was that Kapalkundala, the guide in the folktale, was borrowed not from *The Mahabharata*, but from a Bengali novel by Bankim Chandra Chattyopadhyay entitled *Kapalkundala*.

A question asked near the end of the second section continues to hover over the whole piece. It shows that Bannerji does conceive of a Canadian reader, albeit one benighted: "How is my reader of here and now in Canada," she asks, "whose childhood, culture and language [are] so far away from any of this, to grasp the essence of this experience which is not only mine, but of countless children of Bengal who are at present my age in literate, middle-class homes?" The rhetorical question is framed to produce a negative answer. Grasp the essence? No. Maybe not even come close. But I have a question too: why does this piece so stir me up? More than the bare message—never the twain shall meet—is coming across. There's also a lot of the texture, layers of it, of that other culture. I seem to be transported or translated into somewhere I've never been and should not be able to go. In fact "The Sound Barrier" edges up to a paradox just outside its own field of enquiry—the mystique of translation whose impossibility never invalidates the inspired attempt. "The Sound Barrier" performs the impossibility—hedging against soft presumptuousness—while it bridges. It has provoked this writing from me, for what that's worth. I still don't know much, but I know more than I did before I started reading Bannerji, thinking through and around her text.

Here, finally, is the image that draws the child I was and am into this text:

The book is in my hand. One of the four volumes, bound in cardboard backing and covered with little purple designs on a white base, with a navy blue spine and four triangular edges. The cardboard has become soft with handling, and the paper (newsprint from a popular press) slightly brown, here and there a corner is torn, scribbles by children on the inner sides of the binding, illustrations drawn over by children with pens, such as moustaches on the faces of the heroines and clean shaven war heroes, eyes of the wicked scratched out by my justice seeking nails, and a musty smell. I sit up, lean against the bed, my mother's rather pudgy and soft hand strokes my head, fingers running through my hair, at times the gold bangles make a thin and ringing sound as they hit each other. There is a rhythm to her hand movement, it moves to the rhythm of the verse. My grandmother has assumed a serious listening expression. I read—print, until recently only black squiggly scribbles on paper, begins to make the most wonderful sounds—words, meanings, cadences tumble out of my mouth. I am enthralled. The sound rolls, flows . . .

Understanding and not understanding, often supplying the meaning from my own mind, I read on. The palm leaf fan that my grandmother has picked up from habit hits the ground from her slack wrist. My mother's hand has stopped. Their eyes are closed, gentle snores greet my ears. I keep reading until the end of the canto anyway.

From this lovely scene let's briefly slip away

—To the side of Maurice Sendak as he surveys his first book, *The Prince and the Pauper*. He sets it up to look at it for a long time. He smells it, he gives it a bite. Eventually, he even reads it.

—To the infant Dylan Thomas, falling in love with the words of nursery rhymes, the sounds of which, to him, were "as the notes of bells, the sounds of musical instruments, the noises of wind, sea, and rain, the rattle of milk-carts, the clopping of hooves on cobbles, the fingering of branches on a window pane, might be to someone, deaf from birth, who has miraculously found his hearing."

—To the future King Arthur, nicknamed The Wart, in T.H. White's *The Sword in the Stone*, listening to his tutor talk: "The Wart did not know what Merlyn was talking about, but he liked him to talk. He did not like the grown-ups who talked down to him like a baby, but the ones who just went on talking in their usual way, leaving him to leap along in their wake, jumping at meanings, guessing, clutching at known words, and chuckling at complicated jokes as they suddenly dawned. He had the glee of the porpoise then, pouring and leaping through strange seas."

—To a boy in northern Alberta, Canada, poring and poring over a ten-volume set of books called *Journeys Through Bookland*. Again, today, he is staring in fascinated incomprehension at a graceful line-drawing on one of the pages of a story called *The Tempest* that he is too young to read. In the picture, a pathetic, naked, web-footed creature looks down from the crotch of a slender tree at two clothed gentlemen looking up. One of them has a spare set of garments laid over his arm.

Himani Bannerji, Maurice Sendak, Dylan Thomas, The Wart, and me: quite an assortment of lookers, listeners, readers with a deep bond between them. Allowing for differences of culture, gender, even reality, they are all caught at a formative moment they will never (want to) recover from. They are being hooked by literature. That moment of my own—not that it was a single moment—means everything to me. I've been collecting such moments and sharing them with my students. For years and years my whole being as teacher and critic was bent towards fanning the spark of such moments to keep them bright in adult readers. Gradually, I began to want something else as well, a shunt into the out-of-range, into what is and is not there, not at least in names. "Making strange" in Fred Wah's usage. "Even the varied lexicon of critical desire and possibility," he says, "shows a continuing need to reinvent/renew perceptions that otherwise might reify: defamiliarization, deconstruction, displacement, negative capability, or nonnarrative, not knowing, indeterminacy, silence, distortion, parataxis, non referentiality, dictation, ambiguity, disfunctioning, fragmentation, undecidability, *Differenzqualität*, departure, derivation, opposition, divergence, alter-native, and on and on."

Take one step to the side, you see, and we're looking at an ill assortment of youngsters indeed. To marvel at a moment that makes them one common child across many cultures had better not be to ignore the rest of their lives and the enormous differences between them.

I encountered Himani Bannerji's essay as an adult labouriously trained in literary criticism and with twenty-five years of experience in teaching and writing about literature. If all that makes no difference to my reading, then I'm Peter Pan—quite a specimen of arrested development. Yet one thing has not changed: I'm the same avid reader now as then. I still can't get enough. I know what it means to "devour" books and feel "nourished" by them—the alimentary metaphors are Bannerji's. And experience has taught me to greet any difficult text just as I responded to one that was too much for me as a child. "Understanding and not understanding, often supplying the meaning from my own mind"; "jumping at meanings, guessing, clutching at known words."

I once played a John Cage composition—clanks, booms, hums—on the sound system at home. Hearing those noises, my young sons immediately sprang onto the furniture, off a floor they had silently and mutually declared to be taboo. They enjoyed being half-scared by a troll of their own invention and I loved the fact that they opened their ears when they might have covered them in disgust. The body, through its portals, takes the outside in. *Sine qua non.* Then the "sophisticated" operations of the trained mind have a bit of purchase. "Keep that candle burning bright," sings Emmylou Harris. Curiosity, bright, burning along all the many lines of our several enquiries. How else to make headway with the poetry of Paul Celan, the later Phil Hall, Lyn Hejinian, Gerard Manley Hopkins, Daphne Marlatt, Erin Mouré, Dylan Thomas, Fred Wah, Louis Zukofsky? I could go on. The sea of any real poetry is always strange, no matter how familiar, or who'd read a poem twice?

And not only poetry, though the concentration and speed of poetry especially estranges the trepid reader. "The Sound Barrier" is described in its final, self-reflexive shift as a permanently "incomplete" text, answering the need to tell "a whole new story," "with fragments, with disruptions, and with self-conscious and critical reflections." "My attempt here," says Bannerji, "has been to develop a form which is both fragmentary and coherent in that it is both creative and critical—its self-reflexivity breaking through self-reification, moving towards a fragmented whole." "The Sound Barrier" is metafictional, multi-generic, "open," but it's not a tricky, indeterminate text. The disruptive form answers to an urgency as much of anger and loss as of celebration. "The Sound Barrier" was not meant to furnish the opportunity for cool readerly and writerly recreation; it was written to express and provoke a sense of cultural alienation. Bannerji's reader has to meet that energy of alienation head on.

2

"The Sound Barrier" was first published in *Fireweed*; its most recent appearance is in Bannerji's 1995 book, *Thinking Through: Essays on Feminism, Marxism, and Anti-Racism*. In the "Introduction" to this volume Bannerji implicitly ironizes the figure of the child that so interests me in "The Sound Barrier." First she spells out a shocking fact about her Canadian life that is not explicit in "The Sound Barrier." She looks with surprise at her collection of essays "written over more than a decade," seeing their "coherence of purpose and thought," and also that they "mark a long passage of time which shows no coming closer to this country or the city in which I live. I have spent half my life in Toronto, coming no nearer and going no further than I did in the first few years. This journey of mine in Canada is like an arc, suspended, which has not found a ground yet." This is why I can't go on simply connecting with a happy eight-year-old Himani Bannerji. I retract nothing of what I made of her and those other pre-literary kids, but none of the others grew up and entered a state of social and cultural suspension, savage exclusion, the "otherization" that Bannerji has suffered in Canada. In fact, she is not only a member of what Canadians so tolerantly describe as a "visible minority" but also a woman and a Marxist. Her ten-year essay project involved trying to think the unthought "intersectionality" (her word) of discrimination based on race, gender, and class. Focusing on race, I filter too much of the larger project, but the one subject gives me trouble enough.

In the "Introduction" to *Thinking Through*, Bannerji acknowledges the help of Frantz Fanon in clarifying "the reason for my longing for an oceanic belonging, the mythology of 'home,' in the light of thwarted desires, fears and the sad childhood of an adult's regression." Is this what she's obliged to make of those lovely memories of childhood? Regression? What will it take to ground the arc of her life in Canada?

Canada is a country that discriminates on the basis of race (not to mention gender and class). Except perhaps in official circles, where never is heard a discouraging word, admitting that need not be momentous. It merely means accepting the blindingly obvious imperfection of the country often hyperbolized as the best in the world. I say this quietly, hoping to be quietly listened to, well aware that hollering might be more appropriate. Everybody's postcolonial benchmark is Fanon, after all, that blast furnace on the subject of race. But I need to remember who I am. When one of my sisters makes me shudder by calling her neighbour a Paki, does she cease to be my sister whom I love? If I confess to racism, am I cleansed of it? Not without a collective cleansing. The word "systemic" in the phrase "systemic racism" means that if one is tainted, all are tainted. Let's quietly accept that, without any histrionic self-abasement, and then do something about it.

Unlike the United States, Canada has formed no promised-land myth that might have focused our tenuous but tenacious sense that a new world is a better world. We need to get a fix on the ingrained Canadian habit of thinking white and European norms into the northern section of a "new" world that is in fact ancient. If new is to mean something more than recent, if it's to mean refreshment, renovation, renewal, beginning, then multiculturalism has to be heartfelt, not mere policy. Then critique by recent immigrants will not be met with classic avoidance: "If you don't like it here, go back home." Home? Himani Bannerji chose this cold country, Canada, as some of us never did, thinking we don't have to. India would be no refuge anyway. "I can't say India is a better place," she says in an interview with Makeda Silvera and Dionne Brand, "I can't say that India is not working out in its own particular configuration the relations of international-national forms of violence of state, class, gender—international relations of violence that are happening everywhere."

Feeling dwarfed and anonymous on a trip to London, England, Bannerji says in the last essay in *Thinking Through* that she holds herself "like a child by the hand." She isn't thinking of regression here. She's thinking home, still aware that feelings of "lostness" after emigration produce a "nostalgic search for a 'home,' for belonging in the most ideal sense, as the child belongs oceanically in the body of the mother." "Poetry," says Tim Lilburn, "is tolerant of nostalgia for Paradise." Good, but then we come smack up against the way things are. Oceanic belonging, no; paradise, no. "Cultural orphanhood," in Robin Blaser's phrase, yes.

But in this essay Bannerji does offer a less bleak version of her life in the West, an acceptance not of what she wants but of what she can get if she grabs it with her mind:

> Belonging is often long and painful, but it is belonging nonetheless. How else can it be anything but painful in a society that is built on one's subordination? The vivid sense we have of being outsider-insiders is clearly a sign of belonging. Our existence, like that of others, does not need to be validated like a stamped passport issued by a

national authority. Existential and cultural possibilities lying within our social being are numerous. The emigre condition is in no way better or worse than living at "home" within nation states. Living is simply what it is. It is here and now, protean, elusive and dynamic. It spills over fixed definitions and forms. In this journey we continue and change, are alone and accompanied; taking ourselves by the hand we turn corners, always to become and to be.

This might do as a resolution, if we needed one, but I don't want to stop any thinking east of Eden. I want Bannerji grounded in Canada, meaning accepted in Canada, but I honour her resistance. She and no one else will ground the arc of her metaphor when and if the time comes. Maybe it never will, maybe it shouldn't. "I am not a Newfoundlander," says Stuart Pierson equably, after thirty-one years of residence in St. John's, "It takes generations to achieve that." The same goes for me, another immigrant in my own country and lucky to be obliged to learn it all over again.

Amitava Roy didn't sleep at all on his trip to the United States. He saw over fifty plays in a month & a half, he combed university bookstores for sale books, he watched television all night, every night, so as not to waste a moment of what might be his only chance to absorb American culture at first hand. Sleep is a luxury Amitava can't really afford, even at home, since he gets to his own research & writing only at night. He devoted valuable night hours to annotating my copy of "The Sound Barrier": Bannerji's irony makes it appear that Bankim is a loved writer without much clout even in Bengal. But Bankim Chandra Chattyopadhyay (or Chatterjee in the British simplification that makes Varanasi into Benares, Mumbai into Bombay, Kolkata into Calcutta and so on) was an important Bengali novelist of the Indian Renaissance. How important he was seems to depend on who is reading him, and how. In the notes he prepared for me, Amitava Roy calls *Kapalkundala*, Bankim's second novel (1866), "one of the world's greatest novels." He also says that

> Bankim has been patronisingly called 'the Scott of Bengal or India'—as a historical novelist celebrating the glories, past or current or to come, of Mother India (as Walter Scott did with his country). <u>Controversial</u>—interpreted as a proponent of Hindu nationalism as against Islam. Also interpreted otherwise—that Bankim could not always write directly & openly against the British (being a British Govt. employee himself & due to the fear of censorship)— hence he used the Moghul & Islamic rulers of India as pretended antagonists, making them stand for the British rulers. Controversy continues.

The annotation cost Amitava an evening, but that was only a fraction of the time he spent, with Subir Dhar, acting as our gentle guide to India. On my return visit, listening on the Agra bus to a solitary, guideless American complain about everything in India except Indira Gandhi's house in New Delhi—it was very clean—it came home to me how lucky we'd been to be eased into the place, into a fluid, multi-layered improvisational labyrinth of difference that might well have swallowed us.

I learned in India not only with my mind and heart, but also with my body, with all of my senses & some of my internal organs. I spent two days flat out & dreamy (drugged) on my bed in the guest-house in the Kolkata suburb of Salt Lake. While Marnie spoke on Whitman at Rabindra Bharati University, Subir's mother watched by my sickbed, dozing a little over her Bengali novel. Recovered enough to give dinner a try at Subir & Lilly's house, I ate before a concerned audience of hosts & other guests. Everybody watched me consume my specially bland meal of potatoes, flattened rice and fish soup. Amitava translated his mother's delighted remark that I removed the fish bones very deftly—just like a Bengali. Before dinner that evening, he had told this story:

> Once a Brahmin approached a hut in a village that was occupied by a woman and her children. The woman's husband was at work in the fields. The Brahmin (Brahmins can be imperious) sternly requested food, and the woman, who had very little, just three small portions for her whole family, went to her store and picked out the tiny third that was meant for herself. She reserved the portions for her children and her husband. The Brahmin soon finished the offering and demanded more. Reluctantly, the woman brought for him the portion meant for her children, which the Brahmin also finished speedily. Not yet satisfied, he demanded yet more. With great reluctance, but no hesitation, the woman brought out the portion meant

for her husband, whose hard work in the fields would now go unrewarded. And still the Brahmin was not satisfied. He demanded still more. The woman, heartbroken, burst into tears. I have no more, she said, heartbroken, and threw herself in anguish at the Brahmin's feet. Look up, he said to her then, and there was a gentler tone in his voice. She did look up and saw that he was Krishna. I was testing you, said the God. Now you will never want for provisions.

I take that story perfectly seriously. I relay it with all gratitude, having *been* that guest, that god, though with regrettably empty hands. The story fits perfectly our experience in India. We know we were charmed there. Many things that might have gone very wrong, owing either to our Western ignorance or snarl-ups in various Indian systems, or both, did not go wrong. Guideless, uncharmed, we might have found ourselves in quite a different story. We might have been victims of a dozen different kinds of bad luck or malice. Either way, we'd have remained tourists, permitted a glimpse of middle-class India only—quite different from middle-class Canada in many ways, but almost as insulated from lives of subsistence or crime. Nothing like the lives of the poor in Rohinton Mistry's *Such a Long Journey*. But even about the stratum we were welcomed into, questions arise.

Gayatri Spivak chooses Mahasweta Devi for translation from Bengali to English because "she is unlike her scene," a refutation of the "old anthropological supposition (and that is bad anthropology) that every person from a culture is nothing but a whole example of that culture." (Bad reading: characters in a novel found credible insofar as they represent their gender or race or class, or insofar as they suit the reader's current ideology.) Amitava & Subir, then: like or unlike their scene?

Does anybody else play their game of *Pun*jabi? (The most Punjabi film? *Pather Punchali*.) In how many Kolkata households like that of Manju Dutta Gupta, retired colleague of Amitava & Subir, would we be offered this entertainment: one of Subir's PhD students, accompanying himself on harmonium, deadpans a medley of musical parodies, style after classical & popular Indian style setting the "To-morrow, and to-morrow, and to-morrow" speech of Macbeth, in which life is "a tale/ Told by an idiot, full of sound and fury,/ Signifying nothing." We could catch something of the hilarity of this, the tour de force of musical variety, if not the musical quotations. We could understand that this wasn't Up the Empire, because Bengali reverence for Shakespeare was always equal to reverence for the Bengali nationalist, Rabindranath Tagore. So the performance was play. Subir & Amitava had even had the temerity to offer it as entertainment to the Shakespeare Society of Eastern India & were relieved when it went over big.

A couple of weeks in India—no conclusions. But I suspect that Subir & Amitava are as typical of their scene as I am of mine. Is it eccentricity that seals our kinship in literature? English professors contemptuous of literature & learning must be as active in India as in Canada. Amateurs across the world are closer to each other than to self-serving cynics in their own universities. Here, dated 18 May 2001, at Kolkata, and inscribed "To Stan & Marnie, (friends, scholars, wonderful people), with affection and good wishes" is Subir's brand-new book, *Burning Bright: William Blake and the Poetry of Imagination*.

YEG-YYT

Edmonton–St. John's, Reading Sujata Bhatt

For Cecile Sandten

>*out at sea*
>*far out the dreaming*
>*holds my language*
>*one lets go*
>*far out at sea*
>*so farre off dreaming*
>*lets go, lets go*
>*the words blue secrets*
>*don't belong to me*

—◄o►—

Out of what desire, Sujata, speaking to you—your poems—on this plane, what ridiculous confession—those musicians in jeans in St. John's the night Paddy Keenan played The Ship and I thought why shouldn't I look so trim again. Sujata, I have two new pairs of jeans from the Leduc Cash Store in my luggage right now. The 34–30 tag still stuck on one leg until my sisters whooped, both spotting it at the same time while I sat and sat, mute, on my mother's couch, through the market talk and the farming talk of people I love—reacquainting myself with the sensation of the word   crotchgrabber.

—◀o▶—

February 23, 1996

    In the waiting room off Platform One at Mughal Serai there was a smiling family nudging their daughter towards us. She introduced herself as Priyanka. Eleven years old and learning English in Varanasi. Your English is excellent, we said, and smiled and nodded at the parents and grandparents, now beaming, to confirm that she was doing beautifully. Encouraged, she told us all about herself and asked us everything she could think of, including our favourite flower and colour.

    She and her family were going to Kolkata too, but not by Howrah Express. Good thing we exchanged destinations, because her father caught an announcement that we hadn't even heard. Platform Two, Priyanka translated, and her father pointed through the wall behind us. We nodded our thanks and Priyanka talked on, asking now about Canada. Suddenly her father sprang to his feet. Howrah Express, he said, Platform Three. Come, we must hurry. Nothing wrong with his English. Out of the waiting room, down the platform, up the stairs to an overpass, across two sets of tracks. We were on our way before it sank in, how utterly helpless we'd been. If this man's daughter hadn't struck up a conversation, we'd have sat by the wrong platform all night. We'd have missed our plane in Kolkata. We'd still be in India.

    Another man had noticed us having trouble locating our coach in the chaos on Platform Three, so he asked to see our ticket. This way, he said, and we followed him several coaches back. He showed us right to our berths. I offered him a tip but he smiled and said No, no, I'm just a tourist like yourselves, and hustled away.

―◁○▷―

Bell Mobility has had the run of this nice old DC-9 with the plain maroon upholstery, Sujata. They mined the back of every middle seat in CDE row, every aisle seat of AB row, with Skytel phones enough to jam the lines of Belleville 32,000 feet below if all at once we up and called. There's half again as much leg-room in this nice old DC-9 as in the newer planes. Bell Mobility couldn't touch that. Stretch out your legs, call Belleville, Bangor, Halifax, call St. John's just before you land, call a loved one, stretch right out, we couldn't do nothing about the leg-room.

―◁○▷―

September 10, 1997

In Hannover, I was praising the Deutsche Bahn to my new friends, gathered for a meal in Gaststätte Kaiser, which doesn't sound like an Irish pub, but it is. This was the night before I was to fly back to Canada. I wasn't thinking as I spoke of the Indian trains we'd needed such luck with. I was thinking of clunky old Via Rail, the antiquated Canadian rail system. I had travelled from Trier to Bremen, from Bremen to Hannover on quiet, fast, modern German trains you could set your watch by. If Ihr Fahrplan (IR 2431) specifies a two-minute stop, the train pulls out precisely two minutes later. Arrive 11:15 at Trier Hofbahnhof, for example, depart 11:17. Too much precision for Florian, the student who was helping me with my baggage. Jesus Christ! he exclaimed at 11:17, as the train began to move, his English impressively intact in the moment of stress. His professor's BMW was illegally parked across the street from Trier Hofbahnhof, and here he was on the way to Bremen with me.

I love your efficient trains, I was saying to my friends in Hannover, and no one responded. They seemed a little embarrassed. Then I noticed all the thought balloons with German Efficiency in each of them. So I added, and I hope the twinkle in my eye was bright, But I won't hold them against you.

—◄o►—

February 20, 1996

Touring the mansion Rabindranath Tagore gave to establish this university that bears his name, Sujata, my own internal clock runs with German precision, but why should I be ticking like this, I ask myself, when Subir and Amitava are not? After all, they're the ones who scheduled me to speak at Rabindra Bharati University two hours ago. Sure, I say, invited to view Tagore's paintings, since we're here, why not?

—◄o►—

February 22, 1996

We were dining with Atal at the Hotel Ganges View when the host strode over: Phone call, he said casually. For us? You're sure? At a restaurant in Varanasi? Something must be wrong. But it was just Mamta, calling from Canada to see how we were doing. But how could she possibly have caught us? She'd said we must stay at the Ganges View, yes, best kitchen in town, but we'd found it full and ended up at plain Hotel Ganges instead, with a view of Dasaswamedh Road. Atal had convinced the host at Ganges View, a private guest-house really, to find room at his table for us this one evening. Did Mamta explain her perfect timing from the other side of the world? I don't remember. Maybe she first tracked us to World Literacy Canada, next door on Assi Ghat? A mystery of synchronicity is what lingers, though, that and Atal declaring, in a completely different connection, that everything is predestined.

So my karma takes me to Germany, where I expect to meet German people, and I do, and I make German friends, and maybe one of them is you, Sujata. *Sprechen sie Deutsch?* I've known how to say that forever, also *"Du bist wie eine blume."* Alberta meets Gujarat in Germany.

Cecile was to be my guide in Bremen, but we met first at the conference in Hannover. She had copies of your poems with her and showed them to me. Amazing, I said, I want these poems. Where can I get them? In Bremen, she said. Sujata lives there and she might come to your reading.

—◄o►—

September 10, 1997

Cecile and I photograph each other clutching for good luck the knobbly knees of the bronze donkey bearing the hound dog with the cat on its back who bears the rooster crowing the joy of independence through cooperation of the Bremen Town Musicians. I'm glad you joined us, Sujata, climbing the spiral staircase up the tower of St. Petri Dom, and wandering in funky Böttcherstrasse, though, both of us being shy, there was not much conversation, but listen—you heard Ahmedabad in East Germany, so I wonder—what, in this regulated country, do you hear of North America in my flat prairie speech? "My love affair with Canada & garlic" you write for me in

The Stinking Rose—why how un-Canadian, I think abruptly on this nice old DC-9: I'm (hold the garlic) having one too!

◄o►

"You say my name the way it should be said..."
Sujata, how should your name be said? I lost the *j*, I made it *h* first time I spoke it, praising Suhata Bhatt, her poems, your poems, to someone in Hannover who corrected me. Sujata. And what kind of *a*? Surely not flat as Alberta, my home, whose *a* I can't think right for a name pronounced how in Gujarat.

◄o►

January 2, 1997
    If I may, he said gently: Varanahsi.
    Ah (the conference over, *now* he corrects me) Varanahsi, Varanahsi. Thank you.
    Approving the un-Britishing of Benares, though I loved that name in books, never expecting to learn ghat, gali, Dasaswamedh Road *in* Varanasi—I had blithely been remembering Varanasi all weekend in Jammu.

Say Srinigar, Mumbai, say Sachin Tendulkar. Fine. Now say Chattyopadhyay.

◄o►

After my reading for the Culture Vultures in Bremen, Sujata and I exchanged books. Well, I offered my *Journeys Through Bookland* for Sujata's *Brunizem*. ("For Stan," she wrote in it, "the poems of my youth"), and I bought her others, including *Point No Point*, selected poems, named for (you would think) no place up the west coast of Vancouver Island. (Sujata, I give you Nameless Cove up the west coast of Newfoundland).

Poems of youth? This astonishing book? Only since youth in a very fountain gushes from the heart of poetry. Reading these poems in the air, with India and Germany and Alberta fresh and compatible in my mind, my love keeps overflowing in fragments, including one (rejected) about garlic, about Marnie, *exooding* garlic one night after that dinner with her students, lordy! sharp as skunk, and I couldn't, phew! I couldn't breathe! until I fled and finished the night on the living-room rug.

Settle down, Stan.

I do like garlic, even the very buds of it roasted soft. Let's eat a plateful when I get home, love, and stink in one another's arms. Meanwhile,

> An airline bun, one half-bottle
> Of airline red and Brunizem
> Is Paradise enow.

I have these not very scary fantasies of the plane going down. Holding hands with my stranger/neighbour (his large, rough worker's hand crushing mine). Bits of these pages discovered in the flotsam. Not scary. I'm too happy, I feel too lucky. My life won't be ending, not this trip. The bed in St. John's is warm and most likely not reeking of garlic and the world's most beautiful girl is asleep in the next room.

&

St. John's (My mind lifted itself) was a sabbatical destination (out of London, Ontario), a mere change of scene (& the University of Western Ontario). Anticipated to be interesting (more easily than my body), not expected to turn permanent. (Some part of my body is—) My sabbatical reading (not lost but) was to be Indo-Canadian fiction (still in transit). My graduate course, "The Tourist & the Prodigal" (as though I came not whole) was already advertised (but molecule by molecule) in the calendar.

I find it hard to believe now that I was willing to plunge in so far beyond my depth—India, the whole labyrinthine subcontinent & the diaspora. Two visits hardly qualify you.

In Jammu at the 1996 Conference of the Indian Association of Canadian Studies I listened to several people out of their depth in my subject. I attended papers by Indian presenters completely detached from Canada. You could perform your standard dry critical operations on Margaret Atwood or Margaret Laurence as if they were chosen at random off a shelf. I wondered what had drawn some of these people to Canadian subjects for which they had neither passion nor background. But there was a wonderful talk on the place of Quebec in Canada by a man who had spent some time, but not much, in La Belle Province (je me souviens). I told him he ought to be sent on a speaking tour across English Canada as an example to anglophones ignorant of Quebec, starting at the first Ontario service centre west of Quebec on the 401 where the employees don't speak French. & when he'd done all he could for English Canada, I'd send him a copy of *Dictionary of Newfoundland English* to tease him into the sensitive subject of my adopted province/country. There's another national tour in that.

Well, big toe in the subcontinental waters—that's what I would have said to my graduate students. Let's see how deep we can get, together, because I'm not that far ahead of you. We all know something about the English language & about literature, & at the very least can work with what does travel. Also, there is a Canadian warp. "I am the foreigner," says Michael Ondaatje in his native Sri Lanka, having become Canadian. "I am the prodigal who hates the foreigner." That's the bind we'd have been worrying. & we'd have found plenty of theory to help with mongrel (mutt) experience.

But I swerved to Newfoundland & Newfoundland writing. I found myself out of my depth in my own country. I hadn't expected that & and I needed to attend to it. "In Newfoundland," say the editors of *People of the Landwash,* George Story's posthumous volume of essays, "the 'landwash,' where sea and land mingle, has long been recognized as a rich, productive area. It is a margin, and now in other places the margin is increasingly gaining recognition as a site of change and progress. In Newfoundland, they knew that all along."

It was spring before I fully realized that I couldn't see swerving back & wrote asking to replace my Indo-Canadian course with another, "Secret Nation: Literature of Contemporary Newfoundland & Labrador." Students from across the country were already registered & each had to be canvassed. Nobody objected. It was me they wanted, the graduate secretary reported with an astonishment I hope was feigned.

Z

Burning

Where I came to write: in the rocky meadow above Depot Creek. There was a time I saw the shadow of no parting from that place. I wanted to be buried there. I wanted a big, flat-faced boulder for a headstone, with just my name chiselled into the stone, like those lines from Walt Whitman cut into the face of Mazinaw Rock:

> My foothold is tenon'd and mortis'd in granite,
> I laugh at what you call dissolution,
> And I know the amplitude of time.

I wanted to be laid in the earth, two feet under (wherever in that stone meadow—a crisp walk across the Crown Land to Matt Cohen's cabin, a meandering stroll up the creek to Blueroof Farm—wherever two feet free of rock and root could be found), with no coffin but a cloth covering my face.

> Gee, but the graveyard is a lonesome place—
> They put you on your back, throw the mud down in your face.

I wanted to rot into that gritty soil, that skin of soil over granite. Two feet down, just the body. Let the creatures come, then, and carry me by littles to their own particulars and purposes. All my fluids and substances to serve the creatures great and small. And something of me would reach the creek by the fall of rain, gravity, the circulation of ground water. As a river deltas I would join the creek underground. Something of me would carry down the creek to the Napanee River, the St. Lawrence, the sea. Something of me dispersing across the world, rising also into air. "Does the infinite space/ we dissolve into, taste of us then?" Taste? Not to human buds, but yes,

> She saw the bright sun and, hovering above her, hundreds of lovely creatures—she could see right through them, see the white sails of the ship and the pink clouds in the sky. And their voice was the voice of melody, yet so spiritual that no human ear could hear it, just as no earthly eye could see them. They had no wings, but their own lightness bore them up as they floated through the air. The little mermaid saw that she had a body like theirs, raising itself freer and freer from the foam.

◄o►

> At the end of time there would still be traces of me everywhere—tracked by angelic instruments—but thickest by the rocky meadow above Depot Creek.
>   Traces of us all, secret nations of earth, air, water.
>   Always losing into air what we are on paper,
>   paper selves, paper nations.
> I was so close—on paper.
> Now struggling
>   to order my death
>   into earth, water, air,

    having lost the cottage, lost
    the hut across the creek from the cottage
    where I came to write,
    where my burial was,
    who knows how,
        given strict regulations
            concerning the dead,
                to be accomplished.

◀o▶

That corpse in Varanasi, lying unattended on a sheet so near the market by the burning ghats. Collecting offerings, paise and rupees for the price of wood. Collecting flies. In the evening Atal engaged Sham's boat, and Sham rowed us down the Ganges from Assi Ghat to Dasaswamedh Ghat, past the shrine of Mother Ganges which is drowned when the river floods. Why were bestial sounds issuing from that shrine? Why doesn't my journal mention them, and why has no explanation stayed? Surely we would have asked. Unless incomprehension fixed some invention, grabbed and guided it purely into the terror not to know can be. Then buried it fold under fold that nothing but writing under the skin can find. Mixed blessing: to feel it now.

    Past the hotel with candles lining the terraces of another ghat—beautiful at night but an outrage to tradition, Atal said—to the burning ghats where seven or eight fires were being watched. Sham rested on his oars, and we looked, in silence and thought about those fires as we had watched campfires at home, drawn out of ourselves into melancholy or peace. Fire is not as the other elements, not to these eyes and this skin. But neither of us was ever stilled by a fire at home as we were stilled by these death fires, these evaporating bodies whose souls escape when, at a certain stage in the burning, the head raises itself and the eldest son shatters the paper-thin skull. I was glad that Amitava had spoken of this home-made cremation, this process of the living as well as of the dead. The living also require their release. As hour after hour the body is consumed by fire, the watcher relives a lifetime of association, good and ill, and when the soul escapes, the watcher is freed of all hurt and abrasion as of all weight of love and grief. Without Amitava's words we might have watched those burnings stilled by incomprehension.

World Literacy Canada occupies a palace on the Ganges donated by the Maharajah of Varanasi. Should any of the Maharajah's relatives begin to fail, Atal and Swati and Mamta (when she's not in Canada) must be ready to vacate in a hurry. Holy Ganges is a portal to the next life, a propitious place to leave this one. Mother Ganges blesses all rites of passage, in fact. From the balcony of the palace we saw birth parties, marriage parties, we saw the living lift their lives by stepping into Mother Ganges.

We stepped in too. Swati encouraged us to. Take off your shoes and socks, she said, give me your camera. Standing with bare feet in the Ganges, our Western minds split. Ganges is a goddess, yes, we had no trouble with that, but Ganges is also filthy. Here in Varanasi, red clay thickens the water, but surely the Ganges must be cleaner here than downstream at Kolkata, where we had sat by the banks with Lilly and Subir and Rukmi, remembering clear northern rivers, not quite able to share their peace. Never mind. We stood in the Ganges, posing like the tourists we were. That picture was the only one on the roll that didn't turn out.

—◄o►—

Encylopaedia Brittanica, Encyclopaedia Universalis, Universalia, Encyclopédie, La grand encyclopédie Larousse.

14 *Moyen Age*
ostie

15 ostrava
pliage

16 *plomb*
Renaissance

Sit down to write for gain? I warn you. What is greater than you will come. You will sit down to write and the hand holding the pen will not be your hand—lent to the others under the *Enclopaedia Universalis*. With these you must be friends, wherever they guide you. You will be horrified, amazed until you return. Those eyes are not your eyes guiding the pen along the line. Those eyes will not see what in the world there is to see until this is done. In this day and age! For better or worse with the old ones still! (What I did not come to write today, though gain—gain!—could not have been further from my mind, what was spilling out the second I entered the library, as once we collapsed into flesh just inside the bedroom, too hungry to reach the bed. Flung myself into the first empty desk, in Reference.)

Until today, who knew that I want to be buried in a shallow grave in the Grant's meadow above Depot Creek? I'm no talker. I'll take to my grave whatever I haven't been able to write. I'll end up ashes, and no one will have watched me go.

There was this ailing body,

then there was this stiff,
and now there are these
ashes in this urn.

◀o▶

I liked Aunt Agnes's Christmas package every bit as much as my sisters did, though there was never anything for me in it. There was never anything directed at a particular person. The package was always full of costume jewellery obviously grabbed in double handfuls out of a vanity drawer. Agnes had mounds of extra stuff, year after year, because of shopping syndrome. When she died, Betty said, the house was something to see, especially the basement. Junk of all descriptions squirrelled away down there. The hoard was slightly diminished every Christmas by the boxfuls of necklace and brooch and bracelet and hatpin and earring she packed off to us.

Agnes was a character. The last time I saw her, in Seattle, many years ago, she was reading a New Age self-help book. She was so taken with the book, she said, that she'd dog-eared every single page.

I was long gone to Ontario when Agnes brought Oren to Alberta in her suitcase. Oren was my dad's brother, her husband. I've got Oren in my suitcase, she announced, meaning his ashes, and Betty had quickly to excuse herself and rush outside to find somewhere to howl. I'd have been right at her heels, had I been there, but, once recovered, I would have asked was she taking that urn to the rise on the family homestead near Foremost where my father's ashes were released into the prairie wind.

My father's heart mercifully declared itself all at once on a downtown Lethbridge street. Was he striding down the sidewalk that morning with his old high step? Was he swinging those arms, those open hands that never held a book? Briskly to Smitty's for breakfast, $2.95 with the seniors' discount? He was a gambler all his life and he always loved a bargain. Turning sixty-five was one. Now the government paid him monthly for nothing more than having lived that long. Businesses all over Alberta gave him the Golden Age discount. He was an irresponsible man, but he knew how to walk. I'd like to walk with him again. This time I'd know to hold my head up and keep my shoulders back. I'd step up out of my teenage slouch and swing my arms like he told me to. Then anyone watching could easily see, in the proud way we both of us held ourselves and smoothly covered the ground, that we must be father and son.

◄o►

Mom was laid out on a gurney, half covered by a sheet. It was a shock but not a complete surprise.

Uncle Rudy had loudly nixed the coffin for Dad. A coffin just to burn up? Ridiculous. We went along with him. On our own, none of us would ever have imagined we might turn down the coffin. There's always a coffin at a funeral. Until the time comes, who thinks about a good wood coffin going up in flames? You can't rent, you have to buy. So there was Dad at the visitation, dressed in a suit, lying on a gurney with a sheet over his lower half. Why the sheet? There must have been pants with the suit.

And here is Mom, in a dress, also under a sheet, and Bernice walks up and peers at her and says, You have a funny nose. We were pretty sure Bernice wouldn't understand the funeral, but we thought she had a right to some sort of farewell, so we brought her along for this last visit. What are you doing? she asks her mother. Who'll buy me Christmas presents and birthday presents now? Some of us are having trouble keeping a straight face, and not just because of Bernice.

Mom came of age in the Depression. She had to pester a family with six kids to move into Haig District, 1932, so there'd be enough students in that one-room school to qualify for a teacher, so she'd have a job. She was a no-nonsense woman. After her death she would have wanted no fuss, no waste. But there's inexpensive and then there's cheap, and this place is cheap. We got the name of the funeral home from a woman we knew to be reliable, a close friend of Mom's. Would it be more convenient if I came out to you, said the director on the phone, and Ellen said yes. Remembering Rudy's outburst over the price of a coffin for Dad's, and having seen other people's grief compounded by funeral directors, we were dreading the hard sell. But this man was very considerate. He didn't push anything. As long as you understand that we're in the process of moving, he said. We're moving from Nisku to Edmonton, and our decor is not what it normally is. Well, funeral decor—who needs that? It's funereal. This man said he'd take care of everything. He was very reassuring. Who knew that his funeral home would look like a morgue?

As soon as we located the place, in the Nisku Industrial Park where it shared half a tin building with a ball-bearing factory, we could understand the need for a move. Inside, the floors and walls were bare. There was nothing but a desk and a phone in the tiny office. We were conducted to the visitation room through a long empty corridor. There was nothing in the room but Mom on the gurney. No chairs, not even flowers. Mom had plenty of self-control. She would have kept a straight face, had she been with us. She would have taken no part in the giggling, but the corners of her mouth would have been twitching. And now Bernice tells her she has a funny nose. Not a joke, it's just something she noticed, but a couple of the nieces are on the verge of hysterics.

Jeez, Bernice says, Jeez. There is no way to write this or anything else she says so it sounds the way she makes it sound. She's a forty-year-old kid with a thick tongue. We've prepared her for the shock as best we could, but no one thought to say, now Bernice, you realize Mom won't be able to talk to you.

We couldn't have endured Bernice at the hospital. She would have been in the way, she would have needed constant attention, she would have been disgusted at what we had to do, what we chose to do, after Mom was gone. Taking what care we could of the one who took such good care of us. You people sure are strong, the nurse exclaimed. Well, *she* was strong, Ellen replied.

Now Bernice is raising her hands away from her sides, lifting her arms in spiral motions, raising them up above her shoulders. What could she be conducting here? Nobody asks. We know it would be futile to ask. I can't believe what occurs to me, that Mom's soul is just now leaving, now that her last child is here to say goodbye. I know she waited to die before I arrived from Ontario, her decline was so fast afterwards. I can't believe anything so literal, so sentimental and literary, as a soul staying with its body until, one by one, its earthly obligations are all checked off, and I can't understand what Bernice is doing with her arms over the body of our mother. She's a dumpy forty-year-old with the brain of a small child. How can she possibly look so much like a priestess?

—◖o◗—

Where I came to write I came to love and wished to leave myself. And now I've moved from there, appalled and amazed that this quiet life could turn so much. Sixty years of life, as though a number written down in words could even briefly still this process.

Days when I'm young and fine, when nothing of experience seems to have stopped these ears or filmed these open eyes. Days when I'm old, holding on, when just to lift this arm costs so much, when fingers freeze around this pen.

It's taken me all these years to reach this rise. From here I can see my death. I see it past the deaths of friends, from this good life gathered early into the indigo distilled of itself. I see my own death from here, and I haven't stopped being a child.

> The sun was warm but the wind was chill.
> You know how it is with an April day
> When the sun is out and the wind is still,
> You're one month on in the middle of May.
> But if you so much as dare to speak,
> A cloud comes over the sunlit arch,
> A wind comes off a frozen peak,
> And you're two months back in the middle of March.

―◄o►―

When I'm gone, feed my books, one by one, to a herd of pigs. Not all surviving copies, asshole! One of each. Or goats. Make it goats. Goats are completely sane, but they lack inhibition. We were looking for roosters to photograph that time, remember, and the goat climbed into the passenger seat of my Volks the instant you got out. Yes, offer my books to the goats. I'd like it if my words were masticated, digested, and excreted in tidy pellets. And to the anarchy afterlife party, don't forget: invite the goats.

Sources

Epigraphs: Louis Zukofsky, "A"9, "A" (Baltimore: Johns Hopkins UP, 1978) 106; Thomas Byrom, *Nonsense and Wonder: The Poems and Cartoons of Edward Lear* (New York: E.P. Dutton, 1977) 213; Steve McCaffery, *Seven Pages Missing: Volume One: Selected Texts 1969-1999* (Toronto: Coach House, 2000) 114; Otto Neugebauer, *A History of Ancient Mathematical Astronomy*, Part 1, M.J. Klein and G.J. Trower, eds., (New York, Heidelberg, Berlin: Springer Verlag, 1975) 1; Bobbie Louise Hawkins, *Almost Everything* (Toronto: Coach House/East Haven, Conn.: Long River, 1982) 15; John Berryman, *The Freedom of the Poet* (New York: Farrar, Straus & Giroux, 1940) 342-43; "Margaret Sweatman in Conversation with Charlene Diehl-Jones," *The New Quarterly* XX. 2 (2000), 72; Roy Kiyooka, *Mothertalk: Life Stories of Mary Kiyoshi Kiyooka* (Edmonton: NeWest, 1997) 23; Don McKay, *Birding, or Desire* (Toronto: McClelland & Stewart, 1983) 19; Agnes Walsh, *In The Old Country of my Heart* (St. John's: Killick, 1996) 23; Lewis Carroll, *Complete Works* (New York: Vintage, 1976) 214; Charles Simic, *Return to a Place Lit by a Glass of Milk* (New York: George Braziller, 1974) 25; Robert Kroetsch, *A Likely Story: The Writing Life* (Red Deer: Red Deer College, 1995) 74; Paul Bowdring, *The Night Season* (St. John's: Killick, 1997) 210; Christopher Dewdney, "The Dialectical Criminal: Hand in Glove with an Old Hat," in *Predators of the Adoration: Selected Poems* (Toronto: McClelland & Stewart 1983) 168.

A fine how d'ya do

Marshall McLuhan, *Understanding Media: The Extensions of Man* (New York: McGraw-Hill, 1964) 23; Gerard Manley Hopkins, *The Poems*, 4th ed. (based on the 1st ed. of 1918 and enlarged to incorporate all known poems and fragments), W.H. Gardner and N.H. Mackenzie, eds., (Oxford: Oxford, 1970) 90; bpNichol, "Interview," in *Outposts/Avant-postes. Interviews, Poetry, Bibliographies and Critical Introductions to 8 Major Modern Poets,* Caroline Bayard and Jack

David, eds., (Erin, Ont.: Porcépic, 1978) 27; Milan Kundera, *The Book of Laughter and Forgetting*, trans. by Michael Henry Heim (New York: Knopf, 1981); Daphne Marlatt, *What Matters: Writing 1968-70* (Toronto: Coach House, 1980) 71; Margaret Avison, *Winter Sun* (Toronto: Oxford, 1960); "'There are several writers in residence, named or not . . . '," *Rintrah* 1.1 (1972) 15; Gary Geddes and Phyllis Bruce, eds., *15 Canadian Poets* (Toronto: Oxford, 1970) 266-67; e.e. cummings, *Six Non-lectures* (New York: Atheneum, 1962) 43.

& I'm sitting

William Carlos Williams, *The Autobiography* (New York: Random House, 1948) xi; *South Pacific*, Dir. Joshua Logan, Mus. Richard Rodgers and Oscar Hammerstein II, Twentieth Century Fox, 1958; Jack Spicer, *The Collected Books of Jack Spicer*, Robin Blaser, ed., (Los Angeles: Black Sparrow, 1975) 122; Erin Mouré, *Search Procedures: Poems* (Toronto: Anansi, 1996) 47.

The S.O.L.

Paul Hiebert, *Sarah Binks*, afterword by Charles Gordon (Toronto: McClelland & Stewart, 1995) 7, 42, 152.

Cod Liver Oil

Alexander Muir, "The Maple Leaf Forever," 1867; Rosalia Shriver, *Rosa Bonheur: With a Checklist of Works in American Collections* (Philadelphia: Art Alliance; London and Toronto: Associated Universities, 1982) 15; Dore Ashton, *Rosa Bonheur: A Life and a Legend*, illust. and captions by Denise Brown Hare (New York: Viking, 1981) 41; Lew Wallace, *Ben Hur: A Tale of the Christ* (New York: Harper, 1959) 357; L.M. Montgomery, *Anne of Green Gables* (1908), illust. by Hilton Hassel, (Toronto: Ryerson, 1942) 82; John Maunder, *Newfoundland Museum Notes* 2 (1991) 2; Gordon Rodgers, *Floating Houses* (St. John's: Creative, 1984) 11; Patrick Beaver, *The Crystal Palace 1851-1936: A Portrait of Victorian Enterprise* (London: Hugh Evelyn, 1970) 52; Patrick Kavanagh, *Gaff Topsails* (Dunvegan, Ont.: Cormorant, 1996) 26.

& here is the creed
Halldór Laxness, *The Atom Station*, trans. by Magnus Magnusson (Sag Harbor, New York: Second Chance, 1982) 146, 149, 156.

Police Will Not Turn Handle
George Bowering, *Kerrisdale Elegies* (Toronto: Coach House, 1984) 111; Ed Dorn, *Slinger* (Berkeley: Wingbow, 1975) np.

& what I learned
Grace Metalious, *Peyton Place* (New York: Julian Messner, 1956) 124.

& In the blue
Cindy Walker, "The Blue Canadian Rockies," *Words and Music*, Sony Music, 2001.

Out-take
Elizabeth Hay, *Crossing the Snow Line* (Windsor, Ont.: Black Moss, 1989) 23; Bobbie Louise Hawkins, *Almost Everything* (Toronto: Coach House/East Haven Conn.: LongRiver, 1982) 16.

& yes
A.A. Milne, *Winnie-the-Pooh*, illust. by Ernest H. Shepherd (New York: Dutton, 1926) 72.

Bobs Yer Uncle
Robert Kroetsch, *Alibi* (Toronto: General, 1983) 24; **January**: John Cage, *Silence* (Middletown, Conn.: Wesleyan, 1939) 46; **March**: Thomas Chandler Haliburton, *The Clockmaker, or, the sayings and doings of Samuel Slick of Slickville,* afterword by Robert L. McDougall (Toronto: McClelland & Stewart, 1993) 24; *Under the Yum Yum Tree*, Dir. David Swift, Columbia 1963; **April**: Robert Kroetsch, *The Lovely Treachery of Words: Essays Selected and New* (Toronto: Oxford, 1989) 27-28, 125; Michael Ondaatje, *Secular Love* (Toronto: McClelland & Stewart, 1984) 18, 14; John Thompson, *I Dream Myself Into Being:*

Collected Poems (Toronto: Anansi, 1991) 84; J.M. Barrie, *Peter and Wendy* (New York: Charles Scribner's Sons, 1911) 204; John Cage, *Silence*, 8; *May*: Stan Dragland, "Potatoes and the Moths of Just History": Review of Susan Rudy Dorscht, *Women, Reading, Kroetsch: Telling the Difference, Essays on Canadian Writing* 55 (1995), 105.

& May 1995

Erin Mouré, *Search Procedures* (Toronto: Anansi, 1996) 51-56, 61, 84, 79; Erin Mouré and Bronwen Wallace, *Two Women Talking: Correspondence 1985-87*, Susan McMaster, ed. (Toronto: Living Archives of the Feminist Caucus of the League of Canadian Poets, 1993) 89, 9; Phil Hall, *The Unsaid* (London, Ontario: Brick Books, 1992) 45-46.

the fire that breaks from thee then

Roy Kiyooka, *The Fontainbleu Dream Machine: 18 Frames from A Book of Rhetoric* (Toronto: Coach House, 1977) np; *Pear Tree Pomes*, illust. by David Bolduc (Toronto: Coach House, 1987) 13.

& A Big One

E.V. Gordon, *An Introduction to Old Norse*, 2nd ed. revised by A.R. Taylor (Oxford: Clarendon, 1957).

Mountain Railroad

Bronwen Wallace, *Common Magic* (Ottawa: Oberon, 1985) 12; M.E. Abbey and Charles D. Tilman, "Life is Like a Mountain Railroad," 1890.

& I believe

Guy Davenport, *Every Force Evolves a Form: Twenty Essays* (San Francisco: North Point, 1987) 36.

Les Arnold in London (Ont.)

William Carlos Williams, "Author's Note," *Paterson* (New York: New

Directions, 1946) np; Greg Curnoe, *Deeds / Nations* (London, Ontario: Occasional Publications of the London Chapter, Ontario Archaeological Society, No. 4, 1996) epigraph; Jack Spicer, *The Collected Books of Jack Spicer*, Robin Blaser, ed. (Los Angeles: Black Sparrow, 1975) 61; Ted Hughes, *Crow (From The Life and Songs of the Crow)* (New York: Harper and Row, 1971) 37.

& *Foliations*

Thomas A. Clark, *Madder Lake*, drawings by Laurie Clark (Toronto: Coach House, 1981) np.

Walt Whitman's Niece

Katherine Mansfield, *Bliss and Other Stories* (Harmondsworth: Penguin, 1962) 116; Bragg, Billy and Wilco, "Walt Whitman's Niece," *Mermaid Avenue*, Electra Entertainment, 1998; Christopher Smart, *Jubilate Agno*, re-ed. from the original with introd. and notes by W.H. Bond (London: R. Hart-Davis, 1954) 114.

Typing, Writing, "Racial Memories"

Dennis Lee, *Nicholas Knock and Other People*, illust. by Frank Newfeld (Toronto: Macmillan, 1962) 47; Matt Cohen, *Typing: A Life in 26 Keys* (Toronto: Random House, 2000) 219; Patsy Aldana, note about *Typing*, np; 211; John Robert Colombo, *Canadian Literary Landmarks* (Willowdale, Ont.: Hounslow, 1984) 108; Matt Cohen, *Flowers of Darkness* (Toronto: McClelland & Stewart, 1981) 7; *Typing* 129; Matt Cohen, *Elizabeth and After* (Toronto: Knopf, 1999) 7; Matt Cohen, *Last Seen* (Toronto: Knopf, 1996) 20; John Steffler, *The Afterlife of George Cartwright* (Toronto: McClelland & Stewart, 1992) 155; *Typing* 115; *Typing* 128; Ann Gunnarson, "Touching the Marvellous," rev. of Don Coles, *Sometimes All Over*. *Brick: a journal of reviews* 14 (1982), 32; Matt Cohen, *Café Le Dog* (Toronto: McClelland & Stewart, 1983) xi, xii; *Typing* 33; *Last Seen* 136; *Typing* 194, 15-16, 15, 147; Joy Kogawa, "Interview with Magdelene Redekop," in *Other Solitudes: Canadian Multicultural Fictions*, Linda

Hutcheon and Marion Richmond, eds. (Toronto: Oxford, 1990) 97, 175, 1; Matt Cohen, "Racial Memories." *Living on Water* (Markham, Ont.: Penguin Canada, 1986) 234, 215, 217-18, 228; Matt Cohen, *Freud: The Paris Notebooks* (Kingston, Ont.: Quarry, 1990) 110-11; "Racial Memories" 226-27; M.G. Vassanji, *No New Land* (Toronto: McClelland & Stewart, 1991) epigraph; "Racial Memories" 240; Leonard Cohen, *The Spice Box of Earth* (Toronto: McClelland & Stewart, 1961) 81; "Racial Memories" 235; *Spice Box* 81; "Racial Memories" 214, 216; E.J. Pratt, *The Collected Poems of E.J. Pratt*, introd. by Northrop Frye, (Toronto: Macmillan, 1962) 41; "Racial Memories" 237, 241; *Typing* 49-50, 51-52, 52; "Racial Memories" 217, 242, 230, 215, 228; *Typing* 235, 51; Albert Camus, *The Myth of Sisyphus and Other Essays* (New York: Vintage, 1955) v, 234, 237; *Elizabeth and After* 19, 340; *Typing* 237.

Hortus Conclusus
Lewis Carroll, *Complete Works* (New York: Vintage, 1976) 26; Robert Bringhurst, "Everywhere Being is Dancing, Knowing is Known." Tim Lilburn, ed., *Poetry and Knowing: Speculative Essays & Interviews* (Kingston, Ont.: Quarry, 1995) 54.

& at every session
Michael Ondaatje, *Coming Through Slaughter* (Toronto: Anansi, 1976) 101; Ondaatje, "To a Sad Daughter," *Secular Love* (Toronto: Coach House, 1984; McClelland & Stewart, 1979) 97; Ondaatje, *Slaughter* 129, 130, 133, 140.

Transit
Michael Ondaatje, *Running in the Family* (Toronto: McClelland & Stewart, 1982) 79; Margaret Atwood, *Surfacing* (Toronto: McClelland & Stewart, 1972) 72, 123; Jorge Luis Borges, *A Personal Anthology*, Anthony Kerrigan, ed. (New York: Grove, 1967) 101, 109, 109, 110.

& Spanner/Wrench
jamila ismail and Jamelie Hassan, *Jamelie . Jamila Project: A Collaborative Bookwork* (Vancouver: Presentation House Gallery, 1992) np.

Sufficient Elasticity
John Keats, *Selected Poems and Letters*, Douglas Bush, ed. (Boston: Houghton Mifflin, 1959) 208.

Spanner
Duncan Campbell Scott to Dorothea Aylen, August 23, 1942, Scott/Aylen Papers, National Archives; Geoffrey Keynes, ed., *The Letters of Rupert Brooke* (London: Faber, 1968) 492; Frank Davey, *Post-National Arguments: The Politics of the Anglophone-Canadian novel since 1967* (Toronto: University of Toronto, 1993) 8, 156; Duncan Campbell Scott, "Poetry and Progress," Presidential Address delivered before the Royal Society of Canada, May 17, 1922; Stan Dragland, ed., *Duncan Campbell Scott: A Book of Criticism* (Ottawa: Tecumseh, 1974) 14.

& Liselotte
e.e. cummings, *Six Non-lectures* (New York: Atheneum, 1962) 64.

Elpenor
James Wilson Grant, ed., *The Poets and Poetry of Scotland: from the earliest time, comprising characteristic selections from the works of the more noteworthy Scottish poets* (New York: Harper & Brothers, 1976); Homer, *The Odyssey*, trans. by Albert Cook (New York: Norton, 1967) 146.

Agnes Walsh and Halldór Laxness
Agnes Walsh, *In the Old Country of My Heart* (St. John's: Killick, 1996) 32; Magnus Magnusson, "Introduction," Halldór Laxness, *World Light* (Madison, Milwaukee and London: University of

Wisconsin, 1969) vii; Jane Austen, *Pride and Prejudice*, introd. by Mark Schorer (Boston: Houghton Mifflin, 1956) 132; Agnes Walsh, e-mail to the author; Jay Macpherson, *Poems Twice Told: The Boatman and Welcoming Disaster* (Toronto: Oxford, 1981) 46; Aksel Sandemose, *Horns for Our Adornment* (New York: Knopf, 1938) 301; Walsh, *Old Country* 53-54; Ed Dorn, *Slinger* np; Halldór Laxness, *The Atom Station* 143; *Il Postino*, dir. Michael Radford; G.M. Story, W.J. Kirwin and J.D.A. Widdowson, *Dictionary of Newfoundland English*, 2nd ed. with supplement (Toronto: University of Toronto, 1982) 43; William Rowe, *Clapp's Rock* (Toronto: McClelland & Stewart, 1983) 243.

Twelve Bars
The Duke of Duckworth: W.C. Handy, ed. *Blues: An Anthology*, historical and critical text by Abbe Niles, pictures by Miguel Covarrubias, rev. by Jerry Silverman (New York: Da Capo P, 1985) 14; **The Peter Easton:** Little Walter, "Boom, Boom, Out Goes the Lights," *His Best*, Chess 1997; Ron Hynes and Murray McLauchlan, "No Change In Me," The Ennis Sisters, *Red is the Rose*, First City Productions, 1997; **The Yellow Dory:** Jimmy Cox, "Nobody Knows You When You're Down and Out," Bessie Smith, Columbia 1929; **The Fat Cat:** Robert Johnson, "You Better Come On In My Kitchen," The Complete Recordings, Columbia, 1990; **The Rose & Thistle:** Tampa Red and Georgia Tom, "Dead Cats on the Line," *The Slide Guitar: Bottles, Knives & Steel*, Vol. 2, Sony Music, 1993; **The Blarney Stone:** "The Memphis Blues," *Blues, an Anthology*, 71; **Johnny Burke's:** "Blue Gummed Blues," *Blues, an Anthology*, 126-27; e.e. cummings, *Six Non-lectures*, 6, 5; **Green Sleeves:** Victoria Spivey, "Black Snake Blues," Okeh, 1926; **Finnegan's Wake 1:** "Ever After On," *Blues, an Anthology*, 58; Kathleen Lippa, "Facing the Music," *The Express* (St. John's). April 12-18, 2000; **Finnegan's Wake 2:** "Things About Comin My Way," Jerry Silverman, ed., *Folk Blues: 110 American Folk Blues*, photographs by Julius Lester (New York: MacMillan, 1958); Kathleen Lippa; Ron Hynes, *cryer's paradise*, Atlantica Music, 1993; **The Ship Inn:** "Joe Turner Blues," *Blues, an Anthology*, 104.

The Sound Barrier
Robin Blaser, *The Holy Forest*, foreword by Robert Creeley (Toronto: Coach House, 1993) 181; Himani Bannerji, *Thinking Through: Essays on Feminism, Marxism, and Anti-Racism* (Toronto: Women's Press, 1995) 160; Amitava Roy, *Thinking Through*, 162, 162, 164, 164; Himani Bannerji, "'The Other Family': Interview with Arun Mukherjee," Linda Hutcheon and Marion Richmond, eds., in *Other Solitudes: Canadian Multicultural Fictions* 152; Dennis Lee, "Cadence, Country, Silence: Writing in Colonial Space," in *Body Music: Essays* (Toronto: Anansi, 1998) 9-10; *Thinking Through*, 168, 170, 173, 173, 171-2; Dylan Thomas, *Early Prose Writings*, Walford Davies, ed. (New York: New Directions, 1939) 154; T.H. White, *The Sword in the Stone* (Glasgow: William Collins, 1938) 52; Fred Wah, "Strang(l)ed Poetics," in *Faking It: Poetics & Hybridity, Critical Writing 1984-1999* (Edmonton: NeWest, 2000) 24; Emmylou Harris, *Quarter Moon in a Ten Cent Town*, Warner Brothers, 1978; *Thinking Through* 178-79, 7, 11; "Writing was not a decision: Himani Bannerji talks with Makeda Silvera and Dionne Brand," in *The Other Woman: Women of Colour in Contemporary Canadian Literature*. Makeda Silvera, ed. (Toronto: Sister Vision, 1993) 183; *Thinking Through* 181; *Living In The World As If It Were Home: Essays* (Dunvegan, Ont.: Cormorant, 1999) 6; *The Holy Forest* 159; *Thinking Through* 186; Stuart Pierson, "A Diatribe," unpublished.

& Amitava
Gayatri Chakravorty Spivak, *Outside in the Teaching Machine* (New York: Routledge, 1992) 189.

Edmonton–St. John's, Reading Sujata Bhatt
Sujata Bhatt, *Brunizem* (Manchester, U.K.: Carcanet, 1988) 69.

& St. John's
Michael Ondaatje, *Running in the Family*, 79; George Story, *People of the Landwash: Essays on Newfoundland and Labrador*, Melvin Baker,

Helen Peters and Shannon Ryan, eds. (St. John's: Cuff, 1997) vi.

Burning

Walt Whitman, *Leaves of Grass*, Sculley Bradley and Harold W. Blodgett, eds. (New York: Norton, 1973) 48; Jimmie Rogers, "TB Blues," *The Singing Brakeman*, Bear Family Records, 1992; Rainer Maria Rilke, *The Selected Poetry*, Stephen Mitchell, ed and trans. (New York: Vintage, 1984) 157; Hans Christian Andersen, *Fairy Tales*, Svend Larsen, ed., trans. by R.P. Keigwin, illust. by Vilhelm Pedersen and Lorenz Frølich (Odense: Flenstad, 1950) 167-68; Robert Frost, *The Poetry of Robert Frost*, Edward Connery Lathem, ed. (New York: Holt, Rinehart and Winston, 1969) 275.

Acknowledgements

The title sprang at me out of a paper on William Faulkner by Martin Kreiswirth: "An 'apocrypha,' unlike a saga, world, or even a cosmos, works precisely at this level of doubt, offering a profanely broken, uncertain discursive contest, keeping the boundary between textual inside and outside productively mobile" ("Transgression, Auto-Intertextuality, and Yoknapatawpha," *Faulkner and the Artist*, ed. by Donald M. Kartiganer and Ann J. Abadie, University Press of Mississippi, 1993). Alphabet kicked in after a reading on November 22, 1996, at Modern Fuel Gallery in Kingston. Thanks to Anne Archer for inviting me; thanks to her and Carolyn Smart and Kenneth de Kok for valuable Frontenac County support. Thanks also to Mercedes Barry, Nathinée Chen, Mary Dalton, Gary Draper, Roy Geiger, Phil Hall, Anne Hart, Kim Jernigan, Janet Kergoat, Dennis Lee, Don McKay, Michael Ondaatje, Peggy Roffey, Agnes Walsh, and Jan Zwicky. And especially Marnie Parsons.

Smaro Kamboureli's acute editorial suggestions improved this book hugely.

A Canada Council grant in 1998 supported the writing.

"Bobs Yer Uncle" was written for the Robert Kroetsch 70th Birthday Celebration, Waterloo, Ontario, June 12, 1997; "For Crying Out Loud" laments the author's participation in a concert by The Wild Culture Band, with David Sereda and Whitney Smith, Forest City Gallery, January 8, 1991; "Mountain Railroad" was presented at "A Tribute to Bronwen Wallace: An Evening of Readings & Remembrances," Toronto, Thursday, June 13, 1991; "Walt Whitman's Niece" was part of "Greg Curnoe: A Night to Remember" organized by Marion Johnston, Forest City Gallery, London, Ontario, March 20, 1999; "Transit," some sections now dispersed in *Apocrypha*, was written for "Travelling, Migration, Dislocation," Annual Conference of the Association for the Study of New Literatures in English, Hannover,

Germany, September 5, 1997; a version of "Agnes Walsh and Halldór Laxness" was first delivered as a talk for the Master's of Philosophy class at Memorial University of Newfoundland, February 19, 2001; a version of "Other Reading" was delivered in the University of British Columbia Program in Canadian Studies and the Brenda and David McLean Chair in Canadian Studies Distinguished Speaker Series, March 15, 1999.

I am grateful to editors and publishers of the following books and magazines in which parts of *Apocrypha* originally appeared: John. B. Lee, ed., *Back to the Land* (Black Moss); *Canadian Literature*; *Brick*; *Ecks*; *The Fiddlehead*; Roger Bell and John. B. Lee, eds. *Henry's Creature: Poems and Stories on the Automobile* (Black Moss); *The Journal of Wild Culture*; Gary Draper and Charlene Diehl-Jones, eds., *Ledger Domain: For Robert Kroetsch* (Trout Lily); Jeremy Hooker, ed., *Les Arnold: Uncollected Writing and Tributes* (Plain Sailing); *The Malahat Review*; *Newfoundland Studies*; *The New Quarterly*; *Paradigm*; *Quarry*; Liselotte Glage, ed., *Travelling, Migration, Dislocation* (Rodopi); *Toronto Review of Contemporary Writing Abroad*; *12 Bars* (Running the Goat Books and Broadsides); Graeme Gibson, Wayne Grady, Dennis Lee, and Pricila Uppal, eds., *Uncommon Ground: A Celebration of Matt Cohen* (Knopf Canada); *West Coast/Line*; Brad Cran and Jan Zwicky, eds., *Why I Sing the Blues* (Smoking Lung).

Index

A

A Personal Calligraphy (Pratt), 7
Alberta, 11, 9-27
Aldana, Patsy, 109, 112-13
Almost Everything (Hawkins), 50
Anne of Green Gables (Montgomery), 20-21
Arnold, Les, 97-102
Atom Station, The (Laxness), 38, 168, 173, 174, 181, 182
August, Raymond, 119
Autobiography (Williams), 8
Avison, Margaret, 4

B

Bambrick, Sam, 181-82
Bannerji, Himani, 203-16
Bellrock (Ont.), 110
Ben-Hur (Wallace), 20
Best, Anita, 197
Bhatt, Sujata, 221, 225-27
Bill, Buffalo, 17, 19
Binks, Sarah, 9-10
Black Jack Crow: Song and Dance Man (Arnold), 101
Blaser, Robin, 43, 203, 215
Bonheur, Rosa, 13, 15-17, 19, 22
Book of Laughter and Forgetting, The (Kundera), 3
Borges, Jorge Luis, 147-48
bpNichol, 3
Bragg, Billy, 105-106

Brand, Dionne, 215
Brick, 114
Bringhurst, Robert, 137
Brunizem (Bhatt), 227
Burning Bright: William Blake and the Poetry of Imagination (Dhar), 220
Burning Water (Bowering), 60
Butovsky, Mervyn, 119

C

Café Le Dog (Cohen), 116
Cavafy, C.P., 121
Chattyopadhyay, Bankim Chandra, 208, 217
Christ Church College, 134-39
Christianity at Glacier (Laxness), 174, 178
Chubb, Kit, 113
Clapp's Rock (Rowe), 183
Clark, Laurie, 98
Clark, Thomas A., 98, 103
Clockmaker, The (Haliburton), 58
Coach House, 87
cod liver oil, 22-26
Cody, William (*See* Buffalo Bill)
Cohen, Leonard, 122
Cohen, Matt, 108-32
Columbia Icefields, 45-47
Coming Through Slaughter (Ondaatje), 141
Conference of the Indian Association of Canadian Studies, 228

Corkish, Andrew, 158, 159
Crossing the Snow Line (Hay), 49-50
Crow (Hughes), 100
cummings, e.e., 5, 96, 158, 193
Curnoe, Greg, 104-105, 107

D

Das, Kashi, 204
Davenport, Guy
    on e.e. cummings, 96
Davey, Frank, 156
Devi, Mahasweta, 219
Dewdney, Christopher, 88, 94
Dhar, Subir, 140, 218, 220
Dictionary of Newfoundland English, 181, 228
Disinherited, The (Cohen), 129
Dorn, Ed, 87-88
Dragland, Kenneth Arthur, 11, 45-46, 72, 86, 153-54
    death of, 235-36
Dragland, Mydra Ellen, 5, 14, 28, 45-46, 49, 72, *133*
    death of, 236-38
Dragland, Oren, 235

E

Eddy, Terri-Lynn, 191-92
Edmonton, 13-14, 30-31, 164, 166
Elizabeth and After (Cohen), 111, 128-29, 130
Emotional Arithmetic (Cohen), 117

F

Faking It: Poetics & Hybridity (Wah), 44
Fanon, Frantz, 214
Finnigan, Joan, 113
Fireweed, 213
Floating Houses (Rodgers), 23-24
Floating Voice (Dragland), 135
Flowers of Darkness (Cohen), 110
Fones, Robert, 88
Fountainbleu Dream Machine, The (Kiyooka), 89
Freud, Robert, 120-21
Freud: The Paris Notebooks (Freud), 120-21
From Cliché to Archetype (McLuhan and Watson), 2
Furneaux, Alvin, 158

G

Gallant, Mavis, 129
Gedalof, Allan, 100-101
Getting Lucky (Cohen), 130
Government of Newfoundland & Labrador Book Awards, 7
Grandmangin, Monique, 110
Gray, Théa, 160
"Gunnarson, Ann," 114-16 (*See* Dennis Lee)
Guthrie, Woody, 105-106

H

Hall, Phil, 78-79
Hansen, Miss, 12-22, 25-27, 28

Happy Warriors, The (Laxness), 174
Harris, Sean, 188-89
Hawkins, Bobbie Louise, 50
Hay, Elizabeth, 49-50
Hearthedral: a Folk-Hermetic (Hall), 79
Hiebert, Paul, 9
Hollingsworth, Margaret, 94
Holy Forest, The (Blaser), 43
Horns for our Adornment (Sandemose), 173
Horse Fair, The (Bonheur), 13, 15-17, 22
Horwood, Harold, 181
House of Hate (Janes), 166
Howse, Roger, 188-89
Hynes, Ron, 187, 195-96, 197-98

I

Il Postino, 181
In the Old Country of My Heart (Walsh), 165
In the Skin of a Lion (Ondaatje), 114, 156
Independent People (Laxness), 167
India, 144-48, 218-29, 222, 224-25, 226, 228, 232-33
Ismail, Jam, 32-33, 34, 149

J

Jones, D.G., 110, 113
Journeys Through Bookland (Dragland), 5, 89, 210, 226

Joy Riding (Arnold), 98, 99, 100
Joyce, Jim, 199-200

K

Kapalkundala (Chattyopadhyay), 208, 217
Kenny, Glenn, 9, 158
Kerrigan, Anthony, 147
Kiyooka, Roy, 87-91
Klumpke, Anna, 15
Kogawa, Joy, 118
Kroetsch, Robert, 87
letters to, 56-64
Kundera, Milan, 3

L

Last Seen (Cohen), 111, 116
Laughlin, James
on William Carlos William, 8
Laxness, Halldór, 38, 167-70, 173, 178, 182 (*See also* Agnes Walsh)
Lee, Dennis, 108, 114-16, 206
Lemmon, Jack, 58
Lethbridge, 153-54
Lilburn, Tim, 94, 215
Lippa, Kathleen, 195
Living on Water (Cohen), 119
London (Ont.), 97-98
Lovely Treachery of Words, The (Kroetsch), 61

M

MacLauchlan, Murray, 187

Mahabharata, The (Das), 203-204, 207
Mansfield, Katherine, 105
Marlatt, Daphne, 3-4, 89-91
Martyrology, The (bpNichol), 41-42, 43
Maunder, John E., 22-23
McKay, Don, 100-101
McKay, Jean, 114
McLuhan, Marshall, 2
McPherson, Jay, 172
Medicine River (King), 153
Micas, Nathalie, 15
Misery Harbour (Sandemose), 173
Moore, Lisa, 7-8
Moravec, Ivo, 65, 69-70
Moss, John and Ginny, 110
Mouré, Erin, 8, 74-77
Mukherjee, Arun, 206
Music at the Heart of Thinking (Wah), 43-44
musical performance, 80-83
Myth of Sisyphus, The (Camus), 129

N

Nadine (Cohen), 117
Neruda, Pablo, 181
Newfoundland, 22-23, 166-67, 183-84, 228-29
  and Confederation, 25, 183-84
  and World War I, 161
Newfoundland Museum Notes, 22

No New Land (Vassanji), 121
Northeast Avalon Times, The, 7
Notes on the Paintings of Francis Bacon (Arnold), 101

O

O'Byrne, Fergus, 186
O'Flaherty, Patrick, 7
O'Reilly, Dermot, 186
Obasan (Kogawa), 118
Odyssey, The, 160-63, 164
Old Newfoundland: A History to 1843 (O'Flaherty), 7
Ondaatje, Kim, 113
Ondaatje, Michael, 61, 114, 144, 229
Open (Moore), 7
Other Solitudes, 118, 119, 206
Our Generation Against Nuclear War, 34

P

Pear Tree Pomes (Kiyooka), 91
People of the Landwash (Story), 229
Pierson, Stuart, 216
Ploughing in the Nivernais (Bonheur), 17
Point No Point (Bhatt), 227
Porter, Anna
  and Matt Cohen, 117
Post-National Arguments (Davey), 156
Pratt, E.J., 123

Pratt, Mary, 7
Proulx, E. Annie, 183

Q
Queen's University, 93, 94, 96

R
Rajan, Balachandra, 141
Ray, David, 14
Redekop, Magdalen, 118
Rooke, Leon, 94
Roy, Amitava, 204, 217-19, 220, 233

S
St. John's, 165, 186, 187, 228
Salka Valka (Laxness), 174
Sandemose, Axel, 173, 179
Scott, Duncan Campbell, 155, 156
Search Procedures (Mouré), 74-75
Sendak, Maurice, 210
Shipping News, The (Proulx), 183
Silvera, Makeda, 215
Slavik, Vaclav, 65, 69-70
Slavik, Vera, 65
Slinger (Dorn), 87, 176-77
Sliter, Dorothy Murray, 113
Smart, Carolyn, 113
Sometimes All Over (Coles), 114
Spanish Doctor, The (Cohen), 117, 118
Spivak, Gayatri, 219

Steffler, John, 113
Stettler (Alta.), 13-14
StonedGloves (Kiyooka), 88
Studhorseman, The (Kroetsch), 164
Surfacing (Atwood), 145-46

T
Tasks of Passion: Dennis Lee at Mid-Career, 114-16
teaching, 41-44
Thinking Through: Essays on Feminism, Marxism, and Anti-Racism (Bannerji), 213-14, 215-16
This All Happened (Winter), 202
Thomas, Dylan, 210
Thompson, John, 62
Tightrope Passage (Moravec), 70
transcanada (Kiyooka), 88
Truth & Bright Water (King), 153
Two Women Talking: Correspondence 1985–87 (Mouré and Wallace), 75-76
Typing: A Life in 26 Keys (Cohen), 108-12, 114, 116, 117-19, 124, 128-30

U
Under the Yum Yum Tree, 58
Unsaid, The (Hall), 78-79
University of Alberta, 34

University of Western Ontario,
    93, 94, 97-98

V

Vassanji, M.G., 121

W

Wah, Fred, 43-44, 211
Wallace, Bronwen, 75-77, 93-96,
    113
Walsh, Agnes, 165-66, 183-84
  and Halldór Laxness, 168-71,
    172-82
Watson, Wilfred, 2
Welbourn, Kathryn, 7, 8
Werewolf, The (Sandemose), 173
Whitman, Walt, 230
William, William Carlos, 8, 97
Winter Sun (Avison), 4
winter-poems, 101
Winterset Award, 202
World Light (Laxness), 174
Writers' Trust Matt Cohen Prize,
    129

Y

Young, David, 87

Z

Zócalo (Marlatt), 89-90

Also by Stan Dragland

Duncan Campbell Scott: A Book of Criticism. Ottawa: Tecumseh Press, 1974.

Wilson MacDonald's Western Tour. Toronto: Coach House Press, 1975.

Peckertracks. Toronto: Coach House Press, 1975.

Approaches to the Work of James Reaney. Toronto: ECW Press, 1983.

Simon Jesse's Journey. Vancouver: Groundwood Books (Douglas & McIntyre), 1983.

Journeys Through Bookland and Other Passages. Toronto: Coach House Press, 1984.

The Bees of the Invisible: Essays on Contemporary English-Canadian Writing. Toronto: Coach House, 1991.

Floating Voice: Duncan Campbell Scott and the Literature of Treaty 9. Toronto: Anansi, 1994.

12 Bars. St. John's: Running the Goat Book and Broadsides, 2002.

Stan Dragland was born and brought up in Alberta, and educated at the University of Alberta and Queen's University. He has taught at the University of Alberta and at The Grammar School, Sudbury, Suffolk, England, and is Professor Emeritus of English at the University of Western Ontario in London. Dragland is also currently Publisher and Editor at Brick Books, the company he founded along with Don McKay in 1975, and is the founding editor of *Brick: a journal of reviews*. He is the author of several volumes of fiction, non-fiction, and criticism, including the Gabrielle Roy Prize winning *Floating Voice: Duncan Campbell Scott and the Literature of Treaty 9*, 1994.